Everybody Needs A rule

[signature]

EVERYBODY NEEDS A Mule

EVERYBODY NEEDS A
Mule

The Story of Coach Max Bass

Max Bass
and
Richard Proctor

Copyright © 2022 by Max Bass and Richard Proctor.

Library of Congress Control Number:		2022918093
ISBN:	Hardcover	978-1-6698-4952-0
	Softcover	978-1-6698-4951-3
	eBook	978-1-6698-4950-6

All rights reserved. No part of this book may be reproduced or transmitted in any form or by any means, electronic or mechanical, including photocopying, recording, or by any information storage and retrieval system, without permission in writing from the copyright owner.

Any people depicted in stock imagery provided by Getty Images are models, and such images are being used for illustrative purposes only.
Certain stock imagery © Getty Images.

Scripture quotations marked NIV are taken from the Holy Bible, New International Version®. NIV®. Copyright © 1973, 1978, 1984 by International Bible Society. Used by permission of Zondervan. All rights reserved. [Biblica]

Print information available on the last page.

Rev. date: 09/30/2022

To order additional copies of this book, contact:
Xlibris
844-714-8691
www.Xlibris.com
Orders@Xlibris.com
846213

Contents

Prologue... xi
Preface xiii

1 Newnan Football 1966 1
2 Opp, Alabama 5
3 After The Mule 8
4 Coach Max Bass 12
5 Next Stop: Newnan 16
6 Football 1967–1969 21
7 1970 Integration 24
8 1971–1980 29
9 1981 State Runners-up 34
10 1982–1985 Newnan Cougars 41
11 Newnan Cougars 1986–1990 48
12 Newnan Cougars 1991 53
13 Newnan CUGAS 1992 59
14 Newnan Cougars 1993 64
15 The Fellowship of Christian Athletes........................ 68
16 Newnan Cougars 1994 70
17 1995: A New Chapter 74

Postscript..79
Coach's Corner 81
Photo Gallery 121

Dedication

I dedicate this book to my wife, Nancy. Without her, I would have never been able to do all that I have accomplished. She is the best fumble I have ever recovered.

Max Bass

If anyone causes one of these little ones—those who believe in me—to stumble, it would be better for them to have a large millstone hung around their neck and to be drowned in the depths of the sea.

—Matthew 18:6

Prologue

Growing up in Opp, Alabama, behind a plow and a mule, I always had a plan in life and tried to stick to it. In ninth grade, I decided I wanted to be a football coach, and I set about to make that happen. Playing football in high school, junior college, and college taught me the game and the toughness that it required. Living my life behind the principles of finding good people to hang around with, finding a good church, and finding the right girl to spend my life with, I have been able to do mostly what I wanted to do.

I have tried to help all those I could and to teach my players, coaches, and other students how important things like attitude are. I have this on a card and often read it to remind myself.

"The longer I live, the more I realize the impact of attitude on life. Attitude, to me, is more important than education, than money, than circumstances, than failures, than success, than what other people think or say or do. It is more important than appearance, giftedness, or skill. It will make or break a company, a church, a home. The remarkable thing is we have a choice every day regarding the attitude we embrace for that day. We cannot change our past. We cannot change the fact that people act in a certain way. We cannot change the inevitable. The only thing we can do is play on the one string we have, and that is our attitude. I am convinced that life is 10 percent what happens to me and 90 percent of how I react to it. And so it is with you. We are in charge of our ATTITUDES."

I also need to say that I had a lot of great folks help me along the way, and anybody that says you can do it alone has never truly succeeded. I have a very long list of you all who helped me and if you want to know if you are on it, just ask Nancy; she has it.

Preface

This book was started ten years ago with Coach Bass collecting his thoughts and writing them out on many sheets from a yellow pad. One day while fishing with his friend Hugh Maddux, the tales turned into a conversation about getting the book written. Hugh and Coach Bass put in many hours of discussions and created a large set of notes. It is oftentimes hard to collect so many stories and thoughts, but the coach was meticulous in this as he was in his football. The two original authors did not progress much on the book, and for ten years, the work was not moved forward.

I moved back to my origins, Newnan, Georgia, on March 25, 2021. During my first month back, I reacquainted myself with Newnan, visiting Forest Lawn cemetery to see my father's grave, eating at Sprayberry's, and rejoining my old church, the First Baptist Church of Newnan.

I was asked to join a Sunday school class, the Joshua class, where I discovered I was one of their youngest members at the age of fifty-nine. In my first class, a gentleman in a self-propelled wheelchair came in, and before I could introduce myself, one of my classmates came over to him and said, "Coach, good to see you." Being an avid lover of football, when I heard coach, I had to speak with this man. I introduced myself, and he said back to me, "I am Max Bass."

On the second Sunday, he and I spent time talking football, and he said to me, "Boy, you need to come over to my house and visit, and we can talk football." What I did not know is that Coach Bass had been trying to write a book about his life and his teachings for the last ten years. Several in my class discovered that I had written several books and recommended I speak with Coach about writing his.

Before I volunteered myself, I gave him a copy of one of my books to read, just to make sure he thought I was up for the job. He read the 350-page novel in two days, and he said, "I believe you and I can get this thing written." It is probably not well known that Coach Bass was a voracious reader, particularly of history. In fact, a lot of his life and coaching were influenced by the history that he studied.

Starting in late May, Coach and I would spend every Tuesday morning, 9:00 a.m. sharp, going over details and stories for his book. The sessions would last into lunch, and Nancy would cook us up some lunch when the three of us continued our discussion. As fall progressed, me being a deer hunter, Coach let me spend some evenings at his property known as Coach's Corner, doing some deer hunting. It was usually on Thursdays, and afterward, we would spend some more time talking about football.

The project continued through the fall and was about 95 percent complete going into January 2022. I was at a Rugby match, watching my old team play on a Saturday when I received the call that Coach had died. With his death, it had become more important than ever to finish the book. I had hoped to complete it and have him sit on the 50-yard line at Drake Stadium at Newnan High school, signing copies.

Instead, I know he is in heaven with God and probably on a football field, standing next to his old friend and mentor, Coach Bear Bryant.

With his passing, there are no changes, with the exception of adding a Postscript chapter. Please enjoy reading about a great man who touched and shaped thousands of lives.

The Story of Coach Max Bass

1 Newnan Football 1966

There was a time when Interstate 85 did not go as far south and west as Newnan, Georgia, and the only way to get there and back was on two-lane state highways. Newnan is known for its historic downtown that includes its landmark square with its trademark dome- and spire-topped courthouse. It is a place known for Sprayberry's barbeque, the famous country singer Alan Jackson, and inspiring writers and stories such as *Murder in Coweta County* by Margaret Anne Barnes. At night when you leave your windows open to let in the cool air, you hear the train whistle and the sound of the freight trains rolling through downtown Newnan. But if you travel the country and run up on older football coaches and say you are from Newnan, Georgia, the first thing they will say back to you is, "Max Bass." If there is such a thing as a living legend in this part of Georgia, it is the one-time twenty-nine—year head football coach of the Newnan High School football team.

The 1966 version of the Newnan High School Tigers was going to get a fresh look as it was Coach Max Bass's first year. He had coached at Canton, Cedar Town, and the Boles School in Jacksonville, and upon the advice of some wise coaches, took the Newnan job. Prior to Coach Bass's arrival, the Newnan Tigers, as they were called then, had won just nine games in the last four years under two different coaches. For a town like Newnan, a decent-sized town in the football world of the South, this was unacceptable. Football in the South was a tradition, and Friday nights belonged to the high schools, while Saturday belonged to the college game. In 1966, Bobby Dodd was still leading Georgia Tech, and over in Tuscaloosa, the famed Bear Bryant was rolling with his Tide.

Newnan High School had not really been a traditional power in Georgia and, in fact, was one of those teams you scheduled for homecoming. Coach Bass said, "In my first year in '66, we were the opposition in five other teams' homecoming games." It would be said that some of those teams would regret having scheduled Newnan as Coach Bass took Newnan to a 9–1 record that year in 1966. He would end up beating many teams that had not lost to Newnan in over thirty years.

To open the season, Newnan had not only hired Coach Bass but had invested in a new stadium to open in 1966. Drake Stadium, which was named after Homer Drake Sr., would become the second home of Coach Bass as he would coach his Newnan team for the next twenty-nine years. But this opening year of 1966 would mark the beginning of a turnaround in the fortunes of the school.

Coach Bass took the job in April of 1966 and immediately began to establish a program that would help build the years of success that followed. He was familiar with Newnan from his days being an assistant coach at Cedartown and came to Newnan very highly recommended by former coach Norman Harrison. Coach Harrison saw what Max had done while being the coach at the Boles Academy down in Jacksonville. When Max took over the job in Boles, the school had lost twenty-three games in a row. After just two years, Max had the team at seven wins, which got them an appearance in a bowl. At that time, there were no playoffs in the state of Florida.

The team Coach Bass inherited was a team that did not lack some talent. Even though they had gone 2–8 in 1965, they had some boys that could play. It just required a different plan and discipline. The Newnan Tigers had a very experienced line, and Coach Bass shifted a few players into more favorable positions. He had two quarterbacks and quite a few very good running backs. But it was the Coach's knowledge of defense that made the largest impact on the team. During the 1966 season in five games, Newnan and the Tiger defense did not give up a single point. This allowed the offense to get rolling, and in Newnan's first two games, they scored fifty-one points, which was more than the 1965 team had scored during that entire season.

In the first game at Newnan, in the newly dedicated Drake Stadium, the Tigers beat Dallas 19–0. The next week, they were on the road at Sequoya and rolled up big offensive numbers to win that game 32–14. The following weekend was the only non-win on the schedule, a 0–0 tie with Lakeshore. They came back home, though, and put on a crushing performance to beat Russell 47–0. For the homecoming night, Newnan hosted North Clayton and sent the visitors home with a loss of 14–0.

The next weekend would be a big showdown with Headland, and the Tigers would be on the road playing in Headland's homecoming. Newnan was the serve-up game for five homecomings, and they ended up winning all five. Headland had never lost a homecoming game in its ten-year history and was bringing a state ranking of fifth to this contest. At the half, it was 0–0 as both teams were not able to move on the other's defense. In the second half, Newnan with Coach Bass racked up twenty-one points and shocked Headland 21–6, making for a sad homecoming dance after the game. The win moved Newnan onto the top ten in the state with a ranking of eight.

The Tigers and Coach Bass continued their march of wins by beating North Clayton 24–6 and the Campbell of Fairburn 7–0. The win over Campbell was the first time Newnan had won that game since 1953. That win moved Newnan into first place in Region 4-AA Georgia. On the next Thursday, the Tigers traveled to Troup County to play their next opponent. It was a tough game, but Newnan pulled away after the half to win 21–7. This victory set up the match for the regional championship with Douglas County.

Newnan led most of the game 7–0 until, with just four minutes to play, Douglas County scored to tie the game. On the next possession, the Tigers had a fourth and nine from their own forty-five-yard line. A tie game would have meant that Newnan would have to play in a playoff with Lakeshore the following week, but it was at this point Coach Bass chose to go for it. The plan worked as the Newnan quarterback connected with his receiver on a pass play that went to the opposition's one-yard line. Newnan then scored the go-ahead touchdown and led 13–7. To seal the win, Newnan intercepted the ball at their own twenty-five. On the next play, Coach Bass was just trying to run out the clock, but the half-back took the ball and broke free for a fifty-five-yard touchdown, making the final score 20–7.

Newnan went to the quarterfinals where their winning streak for the 1966 season came to an end as they lost to the eventual state champion North Fulton, 47–6. Newnan though had put themselves back on the map in the state, and Coach Bass had put his prints on the program.

2 Opp, Alabama

If you have ever driven to Destin, Florida, from Atlanta, Georgia, your drive begins on Interstate 85. You leave Georgia and end up in Montgomery, Alabama. You exit off on a two-lane Highway 331 and begin to go through the small towns of Alabama. You go through Troy, Jack, Elba, and then you come to Opp, Alabama. Now Opp is just a bit north of Florala, the town at the Florida/Alabama line, and when you go through it, you better not blink, or you will miss it.

When Max was at college one day, he went to the post office in Jacksonville, Alabama, to send a letter back home. He left the letter with the clerk, but she stopped Max on the way out, saying, "We can't send this because you abbreviated the town it is going to." Max turned toward her and said, "No, ma'am, that is the name of the town, Opp."

Opp got its name from Henry Opp, a lawyer of German descent who worked for the L & N Railroad. Opp lived and practiced law in Andalusia, Alabama, in the late 1800s and early 1900s and served as Mayor of Andalusia from 1899 to 1906. In 1901, the Central of Georgia Railroad tried to prevent the L&N Railroad from surveying a right-of-way into Covington County; however, Mr. Opp successfully defended the L&N's case in court, thereby enabling the railroad to complete the survey and ultimately establish the railroad line, which now passes through the city of Opp.

The railroad forked, with one arm traveling south and the other continuing east. Because this provided a good "turning around" place for trains, and because it was already inhabited to a small degree, a little town was laid out on the site with the encouragement of the railroad. In appreciation of Mr. Henry Opp for being directly responsible for the railroad's existence through the area, the L&N encouraged the people to name the town after Mr. Opp.

Opp was no different from many rural towns in the South as it was not only recovering from the depression in the mid-1930s but still had lingering effects from the Civil War. As a young man growing up in Opp, you really only had about three career choices: the mule, the mill, or the military. Known as the three Ms. To get away from that world required having dreams and a plan.

On February 24, 1936, Max Bass was brought into this world and into Opp, Alabama. He was the son of a farmer and one of three kids. He was the middle child, which, for those who understand, also helped to shape his life. To say growing up farming in Opp was tough would be an understatement. They say hardship breeds character, and then it might have been growing out of Max's ears. But the one thing farm life does create is leadership and discipline. Getting up early every morning to milk cows and feed chickens may seem hard to us these days, but back then, it was how you survived.

Life on the farm in Opp was getting up at five in the morning on a cold and rainy January morning to milk cows and then off to do farm chores before you head off to school. Life was physical and very menial, but it instilled in Max hard lessons at an early age. You had to do your part, or the farm would not make it. It was at the end of the year when Max's father gathered the family in the kitchen and sat them down to give a financial report. "My dad looked at us and said, 'Family, we only made fifty dollars this year. For me, this got me thinking that farming was just not the best way to make it through life.'"

In eighth grade, Max had gone out for football and was turning out to be a pretty good player. He liked defense and played linebacker. But that spring, his dad had rented some land and needed help getting the field plowed, and it was Max who answered the call. They needed to get the field ready because it would soon be time to plant corn.

"My daddy knew to plant the corn when the oak leaves got as big as mouse ears. His grandmother was a Creek Indian, so maybe that saying came from her," Max said.

To get this done, Max had to skip football practice and get behind that mule. It was a few afternoons later when his uncle, Fletcher Bass, went looking for Max, at the behest of the football coach. Fletcher found him out in the field behind the mule, plowing furrows for the corn. Staring at Max, Fletcher saw a young man that probably was wasting his talent, and if there was anything that could change all this, it might have been what happened next. It was Fletcher's words that would stick with Max for the rest of his life and continue to make him strive to be what he would become.

"As Fletcher was coming toward me, he hollered, 'Max, I heard you quit football. I guess you couldn't take it.' Those words burned a hole in me, and if it wasn't enough, Fletcher didn't stop. He kept on about seeing me working that plow behind that mule. 'You look very damn becoming behind that mule, and you will probably be there for the rest of your life,'" Max recalled.

"Well, that got me thinking, and I decided right then and there that I was not going to stay on that farm for the rest of my life. The next day, I went back to football, and the next time I had to tell a mule to get up, it would be because he was sitting on my lap. From then on, whenever I thought about working any job, I thought about that mule. It started me to think about setting goals and plans," he said.

This one episode taught Max Bass that in order to move forward in life and find a better life, you had to have a plan. His plans included football but not just playing. He began to think about becoming a football coach. It would be several years in the making as he had to finish high school and find his way to college, but that is exactly what Max did.

3 After The Mule

High school for Max meant continuing to do farm work, go to school, play football, and work other jobs for money. Playing football in South Alabama, as Max described it, was pure hell. It grounded you up, burned you up, and was just plain hard and tough. Max played linebacker, and those were the days when the face mask was still not in use. But even through that, he still loved the game and wanted to pursue coaching. For all his work, he was elected by a unanimous vote as captain of the football team and was voted Mr. Opp High School. Accolades were coming early for Max, and they would not end there.

For extra work, Max worked for an exterminator, crawling under houses, a flower shop, and a gas station. It always seemed that he found a way into work and into an opportunity to move forward. He watched other young men around him settle on a future in the mills, or the mule, or the military, and for Max, the continued focus to do something more pushed him. As far as school was concerned, he did what he needed to graduate and be ready to move on to the next level—college.

For the first two years, Max attended Gulf Coast College, a junior college where he was one of the few players granted a scholarship to play football. For most scholarships, it is for the duration that a player was in school, but for Gulf Coast, well, it was day to day. If the coaches didn't think you were worth it, you packed your bags and left. Football at Gulf Coast could best be described as a meat grinder. Very few fundamentals were taught, and the way you earned respect was by hitting the other guy hard.

Fortunately for Max, he was tough and hit really hard. In fact, this was at a time when players did not wear face masks, and if they did, it was usually just the straight plastic bar about mouth level. After a few practices, Max decided that he should wear a face mask and had the trainers put one on for him. During the next practice, Max, the hard hitter, broke four faceguards, and the coach sat him down for the rest of the session. "I guess they were tired of replacing those masks."

He worked on football and grades, hoping to be able to transfer in a couple of years. During these years as well, he always worked. He worked at the service station, worked painting center lines on the highway for the county, and later got a job with Alabama dry docks working on building ships. In addition, he had joined the National Guard and went away to camp twice a year. Being in the guard was about service for Max, as well as additional income. One thing Max always tried to do was to be polite and smile to folks as he knew this would help in getting ahead.

Max Bass learned a lesson during his second year that he put to heart and to memory and swore that his coaching would never be like this. Most of the coaching staff at Gulf Coast didn't know a lot about fundamentals, and they were just trying to get their guys to hit and play hard. But Max found one coach there who did a good job of teaching defensive fundamentals, and Max learned a few things. Max thought that Coach Bob Parker was an excellent coach with excellent knowledge. Toward the end of that year, Coach Parker came to Max's room, sat down, and looked at Max. "Max, they fired me." Max just could not understand why until Coach Parker gave Max the lesson. "Max, weak people don't want people around who know more than they do. Makes them look bad."

Max Bass decided then and there that this was not the way to run a program, and when he became a coach, he would search out the best he could find and surround himself with them. Coach Parker would continue to coach as he relocated and became a successful high school football coach.

After Gulf Coast, Max got a scholarship to Jacksonville State in Alabama where he was able to continue his football career as well as work on getting his degree. He had other schools looking at him—Auburn, Alabama, and Georgia Tech—but Max felt that JSU was going to be a better fit. Back in his high school days, Max had made up his mind that he wanted to be a football coach and knew that, in order to do that, he was going to need a college degree.

When Max was heading off to college, he had three things that he wanted to do and would pretty much stick to these three for all his endeavors. The first was to find a good church to go to. Being from the South and from a Christian family, faith and the church had always been one of Max's foundations. Second, he wanted to find some good friends. Max believed and would always believe that if you surround yourself with good people and good friends, you are always going to be one step ahead. Third, he wanted to make sure he made it to the football team. Football meant college tuition, and it meant continuing to learn the sport that one day he would coach.

Life at Jacksonville State was football, going to school, and trying to continue down the path Max had set for himself. But it was while Max Bass was at JSU that he probably made one of the best decisions of his life and continued to say this to this day. "She was the best fumble I have ever recovered. Like many colleges in the 1950s and sixties, there was always a place on campus where one could get something to eat, get a Coca-Cola, and usually have some kind of entertainment. At JSU, that place was the Grab. One evening, Max was there with some of the other players and noticed a young lady he would like to get to know better. That young lady was Nancy Vincent.

Nancy, from Cedartown, Georgia, was the type of woman who also knew where she was going and what she was looking for. She was a majorette at JSU and was working on a degree to be able to teach school. Being from the South, she enjoyed football and would certainly be interested in a football player, as long as he knew where he was going. Max at least knew what he wanted to do that evening as he asked her to dance and then ended up walking her back to her dorm for the evening; thus began a two-year relationship that moved forward into marriage. Max and Nancy were married on August 2, 1959, at the First Baptist Church of Cedartown.

Nancy graduated and began a teaching career at Mechanicsville Elementary School in Anniston, Alabama, while Max was headed toward his last year of college and what would be his last year of playing football. Max truly never enjoyed the necessities of studying his schoolwork as most of his studies were in football, not to mention working and living. Max went to see the dean before that last year with a concern about fulfilling the requirements to graduate. He knew that if he wanted to get a coaching job and be a head coach, he would have to get that degree. The dean looked at Max's scores, looked at Max, and said, "Well, you better get close to all As the rest of the way, or you won't get that degree."

Max got good reinforcement from Nancy as she also said to him that he better put down the football plays and crack the books. One thing about Max Bass, when he put his mind and effort into something, he did it. This would be true of his coaching and being a husband and father. Max hit the books, made all As in his next two semesters, and graduated.

The couple stayed a bit longer in Alabama as Max served as a graduate assistant and did his OCS or Officer Candidate School for his reserve in the army work. But the desire to coach was pulling hard. He would get his first opportunity in Canton, Georgia, as he became an offensive line coach and taught physical education. Nancy got a position as a second-grade teacher and would try her firsthand experience at coaching. The local junior high needed an eighth-grade girls' basketball coach, and Nancy was coerced into taking on that role. Nancy had never coached, but she did play basketball in high school, so she at least knew the game.

4   Coach Max Bass

Coach Bass's first year at coaching was a learning experience, but since Max was a study of the game, the learning came easy. Before the season started, he moved over to become the defensive coordinator, as the defense was where he played most and understood. "In order to know how to call the offense, you have to know the defense," a belief Max had that would stay with him through his coaching career. His time at Canton was short as for the next season, he was hired to be the offensive line coach and defensive coordinator at Cedartown High School by Howard "Doc" Ayers. He was at Cedartown for two years, and during those two years, they won the 1963 State Football Championship.

As for Nancy, she knew that being a coach's wife meant change and adaption, and she changed and adapted along with each move. In Cedartown, she got another teaching position with the local elementary school and taught sixth grade. As many of the kids she taught did not come from affluent backgrounds, it was her perseverance and understanding that she brought to the situation.

As always, Max was looking to make that next move up, and after two years of being an assistant, he felt he had learned enough to try being a head coach. If there was one thing Coach Bass liked, it was a challenge. The Boles School in Jacksonville, Florida, is a college preparatory private school that has on-campus boarding for the students. The football program had not seen much success and was in need of a coach who could begin to change that.

During Coach Bass's early years at the prior two stops, he had come up with a formula that he thought he would use to help his teams win, but mostly to help the young men and later all athletes become better people. His first mantra was "stick-to-it-ness." This was something he learned back in Opp from his grandmother, and the premise being don't be a quitter. Just because something is hard does not mean you can't do it. Another thing he learned was to give his team sayings to drive them to be winners. When he got to Boles, this was one of the first slogans he put up on the wall.

Coach Bass got news about the opening for a head coaching position at the Boles School and applied for it in 1964. He was very persistent and, after a trip down to Jacksonville, was offered the job. For the first time, he would be the head guy and hired four assistant coaches. When he arrived at Boles, the football team had only won one game in the last four seasons. Max Bass knew he could get this ship turned and felt so confident that he convinced two of his current players from Cedartown to come down to Jacksonville. As such, these two boys would now be under the watchful eyes of both Max and Nancy.

Coach Bass had always been a big believer in discipline and believed he got a lot of value from his days in the service. At first, he didn't understand why all the marching was required but later grew to see it created discipline. He liked to point to a character in history, something Coach Bass did quite often. During the Revolutionary War, after the early losses and surviving the cold winter of Valley Forge, the Continental Army got a new general by the name of Baron von Steuben. The baron had been a commander in the Prussian Army, but after his king ran out of money, he went looking for work.

At the time, there were no real wars going on in Europe, so he set sail for the colonies to fight with the Continental Army against the British. Von Steuben volunteered and reported directly to General Washington. Some of what he did was organize the militias into a standing army, taught the soldiers to drill and form ranks, taught the army better sanitation to prevent disease, and had them reclothed into uniforms that matched. It was these principles that can be seen when Coach Max Bass took over his first head coaching job.

The mascot of the Boles school was a bulldog, and frankly, the team had been nothing but someone else's dog for the last four seasons. As the fall season approached and Coach Bass prepared, he went into the locker room and hung up a sign for all the players to read every day: Fido Don't Live Here No More.

Roughly, it means that the days of being someone's dog are over. Max Bass brought rules and discipline to his teams but also brought love and concern for his players. He had the locker room repainted to a brighter color and got the team brand new uniforms. He cleaned up the locker room and made sure that the players kept it clean.

That first season in 1964, Boles went 3–7, tripling their wins over the last four seasons. In 1965, the team went 6–5 and earned a spot in the Citrus Bowl. Back then, the state of Florida had no playoff system, and the reward for a good season was going to a bowl game. In just two seasons, Coach Bass had turned around the program and had them winning. As for all things for Coach Bass, it was watching the growth of his young players and their belief in themselves and sticking to it.

The bowl game that was to be played would take place during the Thanksgiving holiday and would mean the players would have to stay at school. Boles, being a boarding school, meant that some of the players had not been home for quite a while, and since, for many, this was their first bowl game, they were not used to being at school during this time. When the decision time came for the game, Coach bass walked down to the field and saw his players jumping up and down, all excited. One of the players turned to Coach and said, "Coach, we voted, and the vote was unanimous. We are staying and playing in that bowl game." It was moments like these that brought pride to Coach Bass.

Meanwhile, the home life for Max and Nancy again changed. As usual, with the move, Nancy had to adapt, and she did by getting another teaching job at one of the local public schools where she taught sixth grade. Another thing they had to get used to was the size of being in a larger city like Jacksonville. They had never lived in a place that large, and as such, they had to see things differently and the people differently than in the smaller towns they were accustomed to.

The year 1965 also brought a big change to the Basses in a good way. While in Cedartown, they had applied to adopt a child as they wanted children. As those that the Lord sometimes does not bless with capability, those that are destined to be parents find a way. During the process, the Basses had moved to Jacksonville, but the adoption process continued. One day, they were called and told that a baby boy would be offered for adoption to them, and for them, their prayers had been answered. Max and Nancy adopted their son, Vince, and the Bass family had grown by one. With this, Nancy decided that she felt she needed to stay home to raise Vince and left her teaching job while Max continued his career in coaching. It was partnering decisions like these and the support of Nancy that would bless Coach Bass and continues to do so.

5 Next Stop: Newnan

During the time of coaching in Florida, the Basses had taken a trip back home to Alabama, which at that time required driving over a lot of two-lane highways through smaller towns. During this trip, they happened to pass through Newnan, Georgia. Both Max and Nancy took a liking to the town, and both agreed that it looked like the kind of place one would want to settle down. At about this same time, Nancy's parents were aging, and their health had become a concern. Nancy, being an only child, had to constantly make trips back to Cedartown, where her parents lived. Vince was a baby at this point, and Nancy had to take him with her on all these trips. This became very problematic, and both Max and Nancy knew that this could not continue. They would have to find a way to move closer to her parents.

Well, coaching success breeds success, and it breeds opportunity. Max began to explore open coaching positions, and it turned out that Cedartown was again looking for a head coach. But as Max does, he thought about the job and sought advice on what to do. When you coach in the high school ranks and are next door to Alabama, you get the chance to get to know one of the best in the college ranks. Max became a regular visitor with Coach Paul "Bear" Bryant. These meetings were sometimes over breakfast and always seemed to have a lesson or advice that Max took.

One such breakfast was during the 1965 season when Bear had the terrible responsibility of kicking his star quarterback, Joe Namath, off the team for rules violations. While Max and Bear were enjoying a country breakfast, Max asked, "Coach, why did you kick Namath off the team? I mean, this is Joe Namath. Couldn't you have found another way?" Bear stopped for a moment, looked at Max, and responded, "When you have rules, you have to abide by them and the consequences no matter who breaks them. If you don't, then why have rules at all." Coach Max Bass took this to heart and would do some of the same during his coaching tenure.

As Max was pondering his next move, he had another meeting to get some more advice from Coach Bryant. The Cedartown job was still in his mind, and so he asked Coach Bryant for his advice. Coach Bryant gave Max this advice. "Max, didn't you all win a state championship up there a few years back?" Max responded yes, as it happened while he was an assistant. "Then why go somewhere where you have already won? Go somewhere that hasn't been winning and build it into a championship team. Folks remember that a lot more."

Coach Bass's two years at Boles brought him notoriety and would bring him that opportunity that Coach Bryant recommended. The former head coach at Newnan High School, Norm Harrison, was now living in Jacksonville and was very impressed with Max Bass and what he had done. The City of Newnan Schools superintendent, O. P. Evans, was now looking for a new head football coach and asked Sam Brown to get involved and help in the search. Sam Brown was a very big sports fan and head of the Newnan Booster club. Sam, thinking about Coach Harrison, called Coach Harrison and asked him for a recommendation on who the new coach should be. Coach Harrison immediately recommended Max Bass for the job.

Coach Bass brought his family up to Newnan for several interviews and was pretty certain he would be offered the job. Mr. Evans told Max that the board would be voting on it on a Tuesday evening and then he would give Max a call. Tuesday night came to an end, and no call had come through. The next day, Coach Bass had pretty much made up his mind that he did not want the Newnan job. Being a man of his word and believing that others should be the same, he felt that O. P. Evans had let him down.

Later that day, the phone rang, and it was Mr. Evans explaining to Max that the board meeting did not finish because two board members had to go to the hospital to see their sister, who had been in an accident. Mr. Evans did not call that evening as he felt it was too late. The plan was that the board would meet again Thursday, and that a call would come promptly to Jacksonville. True to his word, the call came in, and Max Bass was offered the job. For Max, this would be a great opportunity to not only coach at a school that needed to win, but it served the purpose of getting Nancy back closer to her parents.

But like all things around coaching in the South, the Boles School did not want Max to go. His success had meant so much to the school that they were going to make Max an offer he could not refuse. Several of the well-off men in town met with Max and offered an increase in his salary up to $10,000, as his current salary was $7,200. They also offered up a life insurance policy payable in five years for $100,000. And for icing, they said they would buy some land near Orlando and deed it to Max as they knew that a large theme park was going to be built there—Disney World. The offer was fantastic, but Max stepped back and remembered that the main reason for the move was to get Nancy back closer to her parents, and for Max Bass, "Family comes first."

He turned down the offer, and the family packed up, and with some regret, Coach left the Boles School and headed for Newnan. As they had no place to stay initially, like many things in his life, fate and maybe faith stepped in. Max got a call from Bob Baggott, the pastor at the First Baptist Church of Newnan, and the Pastor offered up their home for Max, Nancy, and Vince. It was not long before the local folks helped Max find a home there in Newnan.

Newnan football had come on some hard times, and as Coach Bass was settling into his new role as the head coach and athletic director, he put a plan in place much like he did when he came to

Boles. In the back of his mind, he remembered two rules that he had learned from previous coaches about being the head coach.

1. Don't get too close to the parents because they will want you to get their son to play.
2. Make sure you put a system in to account for all the money in the program.

The second item was not one of Max's strengths, but he did understand basic accounting and made sure that anything bought was on a purchase order followed up by an accounts payable process. As for the first, Max loved his players but understood what it meant to put a winning program together, and it did not include player recommendations from parents.

When Coach looked at his locker room facilities, he knew that was change number one. Again, he had the locker room repainted and the lockers cleaned up. When it came to uniforms, the jerseys were all lying at the bottom of the shower and had holes and patches. The colors of Newnan had been white and gold, but Coach Bass decided to change gold to old gold and did a deal to get brand new uniforms for his team. One season, he worked a deal with a uniform provider that had printed up jerseys for the University of Texas. The problem was the jerseys were not up to college specifications, and the gold was not quite old gold but a bit burnt orange, the color of Texas.

Coach Bass got a deal on them, and they became home jerseys. However, several opposing coaches and sports writers claimed that the jersey was the same color as the football, and Max Bass was trying to use that to his advantage. The jerseys were gold, and the footballs were reddish in color, and as the coach said, "Many folks don't even know what color a football is when they are making these things up."

This became the legend of the "Harvest Gold Jersey," and Max Bass ran with it for all it was worth. Just to emphasize the matter, he had the trim on his house painted harvest gold as well as many items in the Newnan High School Gym.

Discipline wins the day, and that is what was different about Coach Bass. That Newnan team in 1966 won nine games that year with the same players that had only won one game the year before. What the army had taught the coach was discipline. He said, "When I went in the army, I was in good shape and never understood why we did all that marching. I soon understood that doing it over and over again taught discipline, and I understood and applied it to my football teams."

Meanwhile, for the Bass family, Nancy again taught school at East Newnan Elementary School while young Vince was growing up and Max was coaching. Nancy did so for about a year and a half when again, the Bass family was blessed with another child. Max wanted to adopt another boy, but after a discussion with another coach, he was talked into adopting a girl. The Basses adopted Beth in 1968, and Nancy decided to quit teaching for a while and stay home with the baby and Vince.

6 Football 1967–1969

For Coach Bass, competition breeds success, and it can be said so does hard work. Growing up in Opp, Alabama, was the definition of hard work as farming and rural life could make you tough but also could make you what you are. Coach Bass often looked to the Bible and Jesus Christ and his teachings to find his source of direction. "When you are behind that mule plowing a furrow, you've got to keep that furrow straight." Then again, a story he told may have had an impact on him as a youngster. A very short man by the name of Diggy Boy in Opp created some of the first cockfights that Max attended. Diggy dug a pit, built some bleachers around it, and created the modern version of the chicken colosseum; thus, it was the entertainment in rural Alabama in the late forties.

With the success of his first season in 1966, going 9–1, Coach Max Bass looked toward 1967 with excitement and expectation. What he had done to Newnan football in one season was not miraculous; it was a simple bringing of knowledge and confidence to his players. High school football is not like college or pro football as you can't go out and find the players you want. The players are limited to the district they live in and only come with the talent, drive, and determination that they bring. With that every year, you are going to have a different team, and every year, you have to assess what they can do and build your scheme around your players. You also must recognize who you have and treat them accordingly.

Max Bass would draw on what Coach Bryant had told him about players: "Players can be divided, roughly, into four types. Those who have the ability and know it, those who have it and don't know it, those who don't have it and know it, and those who don't have it but don't know it. The ones who have the ability and don't use it are the ones who eat your guts out, but don't give up on them. The ones who don't have the ability, but try every play, don't give up on them because one day, they will be the chairman of the board."

Max Bass had just about all these in that 1967 team. Coaching kids to play football is a process, according to Max. There are many who want to play, but they were just never raised around the extreme hitting that football requires. Max had three brothers, and as is the case, the brothers were always wrestling and doing other rough activities. Only kids or those who may have sisters were not accustomed to the rough play. That didn't mean those kids couldn't be football players; it just meant you had to get them used to the game.

Starting with camp in August, he would ease the players into hitting by having them hit blocking and tackling dummies or running through those noodles. After that, it was the coaches taking on the hitting. Then finally when the pads went on, it was time to teach technique and then on to contact.

"If you take a kid not used to hitting, he is going to be scared so you have to teach them to not be scared. Show them that once they get used to it, hitting doesn't hurt," Coach Max said.

The other factor in Max Bass's style was motivation. He not only motivated his players but motivated his coaches. Coach expected his coaches to go to clinics and college programs and learn what to do and how to be better coaches. You were expected to grow as a coach under Max Bass. Fact is, during his tenure of coaching, Max Bass got over one hundred coaches promoted to college coaches, college head coaches, and head coaches to other high schools. Sometimes to his detriment, for many seasons, he had to train new assistants.

The 1967 Newnan Tigers had another great season going 9–1. What was truly amazing was that on offense, they scored 209 points, and on defense, had only allowed 39. One thing Max Bass was known for was defense. As one coach would say in seasons to come, "If you got four yards on a play on Max Bass, it was certain you wouldn't see that defense in the next play."

As with high school ball, it can be tough achieving the success of a prior year, and the 1968 Newnan Tigers showed that. In 1968, the Tigers went 1–5–4. Five ties in a season may sound strange, but there was no overtime back then, and there were no two-point conversions. But even with this, Max Bass's reputation was growing around the region.

After the 1968 season, Griffin was in search of a new head coach, and they turned to Bear Bryant for a recommendation. Bear told them they should hire Max Bass. Griffin met with Coach Bass and made a tremendous offer that was hard to turn down, and Max didn't. He accepted the job with Griffin. But before the ink would dry, Coach Bass thought back through it. He loved his program, the kids in Newnan, and Nancy, and he had fallen in love with the town and the people. He called Griffin up, turned down the job, and remained the head coach of the Newnan Tigers.

The 1969 season was a bit better at 5–5. During those years, the plans did not change nor Coach Bass's style and preparation. Sometimes, it just does come down to having players. In high school, you can't recruit them, so you have to plan with what you have got. Coach Bass had plans for the next season, but 1969 brought a new dilemma, and what had been in 1969 was about to make a huge change and challenge for the 1970 season.

7 1970 Integration

In 1970 Newnan, Georgia, like most towns in America were going on about day to day living. Shop owners were running their businesses, farmers were planting, and on Wednesdays after lunch, the stores all closed for the day, and folks had the afternoon off. Meanwhile, young men were still off fighting in a raging war in Vietnam, and the Beetles had broken up that year.

In 1969, the ruling came down from the Supreme Court that schools around the country must integrate.

October 29, 1969

> In a *per curiam* decision, the Supreme Court held that it was the obligation of every school district to immediately terminate any and all segregated school systems and to only operate integrated schools.

Newnan, Georgia, and Coach Max Bass were about to embark on a change that no one had any idea how to accomplish.

To understand this process and Coach Bass, one must look back in time at Max Bass in Opp, Alabama. As described, Opp was a poor community of farmers and mill workers and had poor white folk as well as poor black folk. For Max, he went to a white school while the black kids went to a black school. He would come home in the evenings after school or practice down the same road with the black kids and talk to them with no difference. As he would say, "Poor is poor no matter what your skin color is."

He also got inspiration from his mother in the thought. "God made us all in the image of him regardless of skin color," she had said.

In order to farm in Opp, there were times that you needed to hire extra help to get crops in or maybe to get fields plowed. For the local farmers, they would turn to one man to help them get good workers, which of course, were black men. Early in the mornings in downtown Opp, a man named Jim would be available to help you get workers. He knew all those in town who needed work, and he knew which ones were the best workers. Jim was, of course, a black man himself and quite wise. One day, Max was downtown talking to Jim and asked him what it meant to be a leader, as Jim certainly was that. Jim's response was another lesson that Max would keep for his entire career. "Well, Max, being a leader means being the one up front doing the most work."

Coaching a football team and developing young people requires leadership and taking responsibility, and that is certainly Max Bass.

Another story that is part of Max Bass and his way of thinking is about a young black man named Bobby Carr. The year was 1958, and Max was attending junior college and playing football. As was the case in 1958, there was the Junior College that was white and the junior college that was black. Max played for the white college, and Bobby played for the black college. Bobby's mother and grandmother worked as janitors at Gulf Coast, and Max had befriended both. Max Bass could always recognize good folks and made a point of being friendly and talking to people, no matter what their color. Bobby's mom knew Max was going to go to work at the PX and asked if he could get Bobby a job there. Max said he would, and he and Bobby were on the road headed toward Montgomery to look for work.

During the trip, they needed to stop and grab something to eat. They stopped at a roadside café to get a sandwich, and as they were walking in, the hostess said that Bobby could not go in. Even though Max knew the South to be segregated, he just never saw the difference between white and black and had not even thought about not being able to go in and grab a sandwich. With the prompting from the lady, Max turned to Bobby and said, "Well, looks like we are going to head down the road and find a sandwich and eat out by the car." Coach Bass and Bobby would remain lifelong friends, and in fact, Max helped Bobby get a coaching job. Bobby would go on to be a very successful high school football coach.

When the decision to integrate was told to Newnan High School and Central High School, neither group really wanted to do it. Each had their own culture, teams, and ways of doing things. The black high school, Central, had a respectable football team behind Coach Henry Seldon, and many of the players were concerned about losing their starting positions. This concern was also held by the Newnan football players as well. As the ruling came down with no papers or instructions on how to integrate, it was up to the local community to find a way to make it work.

A committee was formed of students, teachers, and parents to try to find a solution to move forward. What was decided was that initially, the eighth to tenth grades of Central would remain going to school at Central while the eleventh and twelfth graders would attend Newnan High. The Newnan kids would stay where they were. The change for athletics was that the colors of Newnan would remain old gold and white but that the mascot would change. Newnan was known as the Tigers, while Central was the Panthers. It was decided to find a cat in between, so the new mascot would be the Cougars. From that point forward in 1970, Newnan would be the Cougars.

For Coach Bass, this new endeavor would be problematic as he had never put two football teams together before. He had no issues about the black players, as his past has shown, but he did wonder how it would all work out. For the players coming from Central, it would also be a new experience for them as they had not been subjected to the type of discipline and hard work a Max Bass program would put them in. In fact, there were several articles in the local paper, the *Newnan Times Herald*, questioning whether the black players would survive the new regimen. Part of that was, of course, driven by stereotypes of races in 1969 and 1970. When asked, Coach Seldon cleared it up and said his players would fit in just fine under Coach Bass and his system.

The season began with camp in the fall, and it was the first integrated camp. Rules were followed, and player decisions of who and where players would play would be decided. As an example, a running back from Central was moved over to be an offensive tackle because the player was big, and the line needed help. But looking back, Coach Bass questioned his program for that year as he felt that maybe he dropped some of the rigor to make sure he would keep players playing. In the final record for that year and the next, he might have been right.

That first game was going to be against Newton County, and outside of one building, the white people were protesting, and outside of another building, the black people were protesting. Coach Bass came into his office, and two of the black players were sitting there waiting for him. The question was, at that point, would the black kids play the game. Coach Bass stopped, and both kids stood up.

"Coach, are you worried about tonight? Well, Coach, all you have done is try to help us, and we are all going to be playing tonight," they said.

With that, Newnan played its first game with an integrated team, and his players showed up and beat Newton County 29–14. Prior to the game, Coach Bass thought he might have a pretty good team as he certainly got some big and talented players from Central. But there were some nagging issues that would hurt his 1970 Cougars.

Max Bass was a stickler for rules, and if the players didn't abide by them, there would be consequences. The week prior to the first game, the local columnist for the *Time Herald* noted that there were seven starters missing from practice. It seems those seven had missed a few practices, and the misses were unexcused. For Coach Bass, this was a broken rule, and those players were removed from the team. As Coach Bass would say, "I want players that are going to commit 100 percent even if we lose with not as good players."

It was rule-setting like this that would have the players gain respect for their coach.

The season ended with a 4–6 record, with Newnan losing its final game to Douglas County, 14–7. Along with losing those seven players, the Newnan Cougars suffered a slew of injuries during the season. But beyond the record, the team and Coach Bass would consider themselves successful as they completed that first season with an integrated team.

8 1971–1980

Max Bass is many things to many people, and in Newnan, Georgia, he is a legend. Whether it was the stories about the antics of turning the lights out when the other team was getting ready to kick a field goal or removing toilet paper from the visitors' restrooms, it was always something. But there are also many traditions and endearing things that Coach Bass brought to the program. It became known that the coach had two favorite songs: the theme from the movie *Doctor Zhivago* and the theme from *Gone with the Wind*. This somehow got back to the band director, and he got an idea. So at halftime, the band played the *Doctor Zhivago* theme at the break, and at the end of the game, they played the *Gone with the Wind* theme. When the halftime theme was played, Coach Bass would turn to the band and give them a wave and a thumbs up. Thus were the doings of Max Bass.

In the 1970s, high school football teams did not have trainers or anyone on staff to handle those duties, which have now become essential. The taping of ankles, the evaluation of injuries, the facilitation of the whirlpools, and the proper application of ice have all become part of the sport. In 1974, Coach Max Bass had seen the positive effects of having such a person, and he began to look for someone to take the role.

Harry Mullins was attending Southern Mississippi, the same school Max would go to later, and Harry was told by Coach Mike Parker that Newnan was looking for a trainer. Max and Harry spoke, and Harry decided to take a trip to Newnan to see what the job would entail. When Harry got to Newnan, he found the only equipment for him was a first aid kit with NHS spray painted on the outside. Still, Harry took the job and set about trying to get the proper equipment needed.

It was determined that a whirlpool was needed, and Harry went into Coach Bass's office to speak with him. "Max, we need a whirlpool," to which Max responded, "We ain't got no money." But like all good leaders, Coach Bass got a local guy, Sam Brown, to build one. Three weeks later, the Newnan High School had a custom-built whirlpool. The need for a cold tub was met by local Coca-Cola that gave Harry one of those old-fashioned coke boxes that held water and ice. When players sat in it, they knew it was from Coke because the emblem was still on the side.

Coach Bass saw the value of having a trainer as his players recovered faster and were better prepared. In fact, Newnan was the first high school football team in Georgia to have a trainer, and as such, other local teams began to send players to Harry for recovery and care.

Harry stepped down from his position in 1981 and was replaced by James "Radar" Brantley who would be the head trainer for Newnan for the next thirty-five years. He still volunteers time at Newnan football games and is a frequent visitor at Coach's Corner, the home of Max Bass.

The 1971 season brought a 5–5 record as Coach Bass struggled with a new issue. When it came to drug use, Coach had a strict rule: if you use it or are around others that do, you are off the team. As he believed in life, he told his players, "Find good people to hang around with, and your life will be better." Dope and marijuana got several of his players kicked off the team. Another change that made things a bit harder was the introduction of black students in 1970. The school grew, which meant that they moved up to the more competitive ranks of AAA football versus AA. The competition was going to be better.

In the 1972 campaign, the Cougars turned a corner going 7–2–1, and lost the first game of the regional to their rival Griffin. From 1972 to 1980, the Cougars would have winning seasons, seven out of those nine years. In 1977, Coach Bass posted a 10-win season, the first 10-win season in Newnan football history.

In 1974, Max decided to get a master's degree in athletic administration and did so at the University of Southern Mississippi. As usual, when Southern Mississippi saw the quality of Coach, they offered him a job on their staff, and of course, Max turned it down in order to stay with his beloved Newnan. Coach Bass was the head of all athletics while at Newnan and saw to it that not only his football players were taken care of, but all the sports and participants were. When he saw that some of the girls on the track team took a licking to their warmup sweats, he made sure they could keep them at the end of the season.

Doing things like making the athletes happy went a long way in the community. Coach Bass made sure that the town was behind his school and really used the boosters to make sure that the whole program was a well-oiled machine. Local businesses bought ads in the program and sponsored different athletic groups. Coach Bass made sure that the cheerleaders were involved not only in the cheering but also in the motivation. One year, Coach Bass met with the head coach of the University of Baylor, Grant Teaff, at a clinic, and they had a discussion on motivation. Coach Teaff talked about how he had a bunch of gold dots made up, and for every great play, a player got a dot to put on his helmet. Max Bass was never one not to take a good idea from someone else and run with it, so he returned to Newnan and got to punching gold dots from helmet tape. From this, a slogan arose on the team, "Dot Em."

If you ever watch a high school game and many college games, you often see the players run out onto the field and break through a big paper sign. Usually, this sign will say something about the opposition and some other point of motivation. This one particular year, the cheerleaders came to Coach Bass and asked him what they should put on the banner for the next game. In his usual Max Bass way, he told them, "Just put dot em. They will know what that means." That Friday night, the team ran onto the field through a banner that had written on it DOT EM.

Team motivation was a common theme as Coach would hang signs with sayings in the locker room, the bathroom, etc. But what he was really known for was defense. He was prouder if his team shutout another team than if they scored six or seven touchdowns. Max had played defense most of his playing days and realized that it was probably the most important aspect of the game. Since he also called all the offensive plays, he held that in order to play good offense, you better know defense so you know where and how to attack the other team. Coach Bass would send his plays in with a messenger system, which meant a player would be sent in with the play to the huddle, while his counterpart came out to be ready to send in the next play. Back in the seventies, this was very common and is still in use by some coaches today. In one such game, the Cougars got several delay-of-game penalties called because Coach Bass was taking time to see what the opposing defense was setting up before he called the play. This also required that his messengers, two co-starting running backs had to sprint to the huddle to deliver the play, which in turn meant that late in the game, these players were more tired. This actually was used by a lot of coaches who learned it was better to shuttle in plays with wide receivers because they usually lined up closer to the sideline and, at times, were less involved.

Also, during this period, many teams were running Wishbone, Veer, and I formations that leaned to more option football. Passing was there but not like it is today. Defensive formations were either five- or six-man fronts—five-man defined as a base fifty defense or, by some, a five two, meaning five down lineman and two line backers. Coach Bass would then send in a defensive play call using three numbers. Each number meant something different to the guard, the tackles, and the linebackers. It simplified what his players had to do and allowed them to attack the offense with aggression and speed rather than having to slow down and think through the play.

In 1975, the Newnan Cougars posted an eight-and-three record and made it to the regional playoffs of 6AAA where they lost. But a trend in success was being set. In 1977, they went 10–2 before losing in the quarterfinals of the 6AAA regional playoffs. In 1978, the 9–3 Cougars again went to the regional playoff where they lost the first game. And as is with high school football, the next two seasons were not successful, with Newnan going 3–7 followed by a 5–5 season. But the 1981 season would be a season to remember.

9   1981 State Runners-up

Coach Bass likes to portray himself as just a country boy from Opp who is just bright enough to get by. The fact is that this is further from the truth than one can imagine. While in his younger days, he did not crack the books like he should and did not read as much as he should. He changed direction on this and began to study more than football. He took to studying military men, successful businessmen, and motivational coaches.

One day, the Newnan principal, Alan Woods, walked into Coach Bass's office and noticed the book the coach had been reading lying on the desk. The book was about the techniques of Attila the Hun. What Coach Bass learned from this is not certain as it was either how he devised the player enlightenment of running wind sprints up the hill next to the field or the principles of discipline that were applied to his coaching style.

Coach also liked to say that his success would have never been possible without great folks to help him. Besides assistant coaches, his greatest support and help came from his secretary, Betty Rogers. Betty was the secretary from 1971–1992. and her main job was to keep the office and the coach organized. One day, Vince Dooley, the University of Georgia head coach came into the office and asked about a couple of players he was recruiting. In minutes, all the information he needed about both kids was in his hands, and he commented that he had never seen a more organized operation.

After 1992, when Betty stepped down from her role, Coach Bass said that her leaving was the biggest blow to his team than any other person who had ever left.

The 1981 season was going to have its challenges, playing some tough foes and rebounding from two subpar seasons. The team, though, had many experienced starters and leaders who would help push toward success. The first game was against Columbus, and the Cougars smothered the opposition, 43–8. The team would go on to win its first five games, and with its fifth victory, 21–0 over Forest Park, Max Bass had reached the one-hundredth win of his career. But what else that win brought the team was a ranking of sixth in the state in AAAA. After, the 1977 season moved up into the tougher AAAA as a result of the increase in the size of the school.

Never stop learning is always how Coach Max Bass worked his profession. He would attend many coaching clinics as a participant and as a speaker. During one chance visit at a clinic, he met Paul Johnson, the former head coach at Georgia Tech, Navy, and Georgia Southern, where he won two national championships.

At the time, Coach Johnson was the offensive coordinator for the Hawaii Rainbow Warriors. As often as was the case, Max told Coach Johnson that he had never been to Hawaii and would entertain a visit. A few weeks later, Max got a call from Coach Johnson that the trip was set, and that Max would be a speaker at the clinic taking place there. As was always the case, Nancy was going along for the trip, and as such, the Basses got a trip to Hawaii.

But clinics and trips were not all about vacations for Coach Bass. He met many coaches and learned about the offensive systems they ran and the defense. One such visit took him to Delaware, the home of the single-wing offense. Coach Bass would utilize this form of attack in his offenses during his tenure.

Motivation and getting players and coaches motivated were some things Max learned from Coach Bear Bryant and a clinic that was attended by Fred Akers, which brought new thoughts and practice to Max. Coach Akers had gone to Wyoming to be the head coach of the Cowboys and, in his first year, went 3–8. Wyoming has always been a challenging place to coach, and for Fred Akers, it was no exception. The next year, Wyoming went 8–3 and played against Oklahoma in the Fiesta Bowl. Coach Bass asked Fred how he got that program turned around so fast, and Fred explained to him that he got his players motivated. He got them motivated by bringing in a motivational coach, Lou Tice.

With this information, Coach Bass did what he always does, picked up the phone, and called Lou. He figured there couldn't be many Lou Tices in the Seattle area, so he looked him up. Lou took Coach Bass's call, and the two of them made a plan to meet up. Lou was going to Florida to do a speech in prison, and that would be the first meeting. But plans changed as that was canceled, and Lou said they could meet in Atlanta. The two coaches met, and Lou provided advice to coach and improvements on motivation. This would go a long way in what happened in 1981.

After the 5–0 start, the Newnan Cougars were next going to face one of their rivals in the Griffin Bears. Griffin was considered the top team in regional 6AAA ball and brought in confidence, as the year before, they had smothered Newnan 56–6. But Lloyd Bohannon, the Griffin coach, had watched the films and said that Newnan was a different team than the prior year. Newnan's defense had vastly improved, and they were playing with great confidence.

An overflowing crowd came to Drake Stadium to see what was being tabbed as the number one game being played in the State of Georgia that night. The home crowd had much to cheer about as Newnan scored late in the second quarter to take a fourteen-to-nothing lead into the locker room. It looked like Newnan was going to walk away with the game, as in the third quarter, they marched down the field into scoring position. But four tries ended at the Griffin two-yard line, and the Bears went on their own march and scored, making the game still in Newnan's favor, 14–7.

In the fourth quarter, Newnan fumbled on their own twenty, and Griffin was in business. They went on to score a touchdown but then missed the extra point, leaving Newnan up 14–13. Newnan failed to move the football, and Griffin took over with enough time to score and win. They moved the ball down to the Newnan nine, but lady luck and good defense were with Newnan that night as a late interception kept the Bears out, and the game ended with a Cougar victory.

At this point in the season, all the talk was about Coach Bass and achieving his first perfect regular season. With two games to go and against two tough opponents, Max was not listening to any of it. His mind was focused on the next opponent and keeping his players focused. The Cougars won the next game against Morrow, 16–0, in what was described as a bruising contest and were ready to seal the undefeated regular season. Newnan had clinched a spot in the playoffs the game before, and as always with teams, this became a challenge to stay focused on finishing.

The final game was a road trip to play 8–1 La Grange, a very tough matchup. Both teams featured solid defenses, and both teams ran their base offense out of the Wing-T. But as Coach Bass would say, when you are assured of something, it is hard to stay up and focused. The Cougars went into Granger land and walked away with a loss, 25–7. So ended the chance for the perfect undefeated regular season.

But as can happen, the game would be played again, as LaGrange and Newnan would square off in a first-round playoff game to determine the 6AAAA champion. Max Bass knew it would be a tough game, but he also knew that beating a team twice in the same season was difficult, and he played off that with his players to get them ready. In the rematch, the Newnan Cougars blanked the LaGrange Grangers 21–0 to win the 6AAAA region and advance to the playoffs. After the game, Coach Bass had this to say, "The difference between this game and that one, the loss, is that the first one didn't count. It's hard beating a team twice in this region. You best yourself trying."

Douglas County would be the next opponent, and they had Max worried as they were a big string team that ran at you out of the I formation. Douglas County was coming in with a 10–1 record and was ready to play. The game went badly for the Cougars as Douglas County jumped into a 21–0 lead at the half. But Douglas County was starting to show fatigue as they had seven or eight players who played both ways, and that was just hard to do in AAAA football. In the second half, Newnan came out and dominated both on offense and defense. They shut out Douglas County in the second half and scored twenty-two points to win the game.

Next up was the North Georgia Championship and a game with a 10–2 Peachtree High. Peachtree's strength was in a sophomore quarterback who had an arm and wits to make this game quite a challenge for the Cougars. For Newnan, it was all about speed, as their two running backs, Warren Newson and Joe Reese, had both clocked 4.4 seconds forty times.

There were times when Newnan won games during the year with punt returns or end-around instead of sustained drives, and this had some of the fans worried. A long-time Newnan supporter came up to Coach Bass and asked, "I'm kinda worried, Coach. We didn't have as many first downs as the other teams." Coach Bass turned to him, "Hoss, look up at that scoreboard. Do you see any place to put first downs?" Hoss was a term Coach Bass often used when addressing people, and in turn, many took up the name and used it when addressing Coach Bass.

All the prognosticators figured this would be a game featuring high-powered offense, something Coach Bass rarely relied on and did not prefer. But he knew that the passing attack of Peachtree was going to be a big challenge. The game started at 8:01 p.m. at Dekalb Memorial Stadium and was all but over by 8:17. The Newnan Cougars caused the first turnover, which was followed up by a 41-yard touchdown. The next series for Peachtree went just two plays before Bass's defense intercepted a pass and took over the ball. The drive took seven plays to put it in, but it resulted in another Newnan touchdown. Peachtree's next drive was stopped after one first down, and Newnan took three plays to cover the distance. In sixteen minutes of time, not game time, Newnan was up 21–0. What was supposed to be an offensive showdown was that way for only one team, and that team was coached by Max Bass. He had his defense prepared, and it showed.

Newnan would score again before the half and take a 28–0 lead into the locker room. Newnan came out and scored again to gain a 35–0 lead in the second half. But other than three second-half touchdowns for Peachtree, two late in the game, Newnan had become the North Georgia AAAA champion and would face the South champions the next week.

After the game, Coach Bass had great compliments for his one-two punch of both his running backs, as both had eclipsed the one-thousand-yard mark for the season. "I wouldn't trade that combination for any two in the state. They are both super football players, but more important, they are two fine young men and solid team players. And what I like most about both of them is that they will be back next year because they are juniors."

Warner Robbins was going to be the opponent as they were the 2AAAA champions and had won the South Georgia AAAA championship by defeating Coffee County. Warner Robbins was bringing a record of 14–0 and liked running the ball straight at the opposition and overpowering them. This would be no easy task for Coach Bass, even with "The Max Bass Edge."

Sometimes, some stories are lore made up to enhance reality, and sometimes, the stories aren't really the way they happened, but some of the coaches around the State of Georgia believed that Max Bass did things to give his team the edge. One such story told was that Coach Bass had all the toilet paper removed from the opposing team's dressing room. This would force the team to go without or ask Newnan for toilet paper, believing this was some kind of psychological edge given to Newnan.

Another time, the opposing team was lining up for a game-winning field goal when the lights went out. In the end, they kicked the field goal. The ref told the coach he could either wait for the lights to go back on, or they could switch end zones and kick. The coach decided to switch end zones, and the kicker, the coach's son, missed the thirty-two-yard field goal.

The game was played in Newnan at Drake Stadium, and the crowd was overflowing and ready. But for Newnan, it would not turn out to be a victory as Warner Robbins brought its full weight down on the Cougars and won the game, 21–0. Newnan just could not move the ball on Warner Robbins, and as it turned out, one of their star running backs was unable to play as he had hurt his ankle in the previous game. In the second quarter, his replacement went out injured as well, and the Newnan running game disappeared. Coach Bass has said excuses are for losers, and he would not use the loss of players as an excuse. His team played hard, but in the end, it was not enough.

Newnan finished the season 13–2 and was runner-up state champion. They had won their region and the North half of the state, but the one they wanted the most got away. At the end of the season, Coach Bass pointed to his team and said that the team was not loaded with division 1 college talent, but they played as a team. He also pointed to his seventeen seniors as leaders and said they would be missed for the next season. There was much anticipation for the 1982 Newnan Cougars as they returned many of their weapons; however, they lost a good number of offensive linemen, and that position would be the question mark.

10 1982–1985 Newnan Cougars

Max Bass was the kind of head coach who was always looking for an edge over the other team. Of course, he was accused of having jerseys the color of the football, having the lights go out on one end of the field where the opposition was to try and kick the winning field goal, and locking the opposing teams in the visitors' locker room at halftime. One interesting story is that before one game, he wanted his assistant coaches to go out and get him a goat to put on the sidelines. His coaches asked Max why. "What would we be doing with that goat," they asked. Max looked at them and said, "See, if you are asking that, think about the coaches on the other sideline. They will be busy thinking about that goat instead of the game." He did not follow through, but it goes down in another Max Bass legendary story. The Max Bass edge.

Coach Bass will also tell you, "High school football is not like college or the pros. You can't go out and recruit players like college, and you can't go out and buy players like the pros. You can only work with what mama drops, and that can be different every year." After the 1981 season and the state championship loss, Newnan looked to be set to maybe make another run for it in 1982. They returned their one-two punch at running back and a good many of the rest of the team. What was missing was the seventeen seniors from the previous year and some key positions at the offensive line.

When you have as successful a season as 1981 was, the expectations only grow larger for the next season. A strong defense was returning as well as two-thousand-yard running backs, but what Coach Bass saw was that he had to replace most of the offensive line. Football has not changed in one hundred years, and it is truly all about blocking and tackling. You can have the greatest running back there is, but if you don't have a good offensive line, you are not going to have great success.

The 1982 season started with a nice win over Columbus 28–0 and was a hallmark defensive game that Coach Bass was known for. The season had the usual cast of opponents—LaGrange and Griffin—and as such, it was going to be challenging. By mid-season, Newnan had a 4–1 record and looked to be having another good year. They would stumble in two more games, including a loss to LaGrange but finish the regular season with a win and a very good 7–3 record that got them in the playoffs. Who was the opponent? Well, of course, La Grange. It seems that most Newnan seasons face LA Grange twice, and as Coach Bass would say, "It is the second one that counts." The game was a hard-fought defensive struggle, but the Newnan Cougars' season would end with a 10–7 loss.

The 1983 season was just about a carbon copy of the previous season. The cougars finished 7–4 with a loss in the regional playoff. The 1984 season started with the usual concerns of having new faces and trying to figure out how best to use them. Newnan had always been known as a running football team as Coach Bass did not like to throw it unless he had better than average chances to catch the ball. Max, being a student of Bear Bryant, had much the same philosophy about the passing game. As the Bear said, "When you throw the ball, three things can happen, and only one of them is good."

Newnan this year had a quarterback who was a pretty good player and a good passer, Johnny Cash. With Cash as the quarterback, Coach Bass had more options for his offense, and he felt pretty good about the upcoming season.

High school football is not pro football or college. You play with your best, regardless of what size they are. To put it in perspective of what Coach Bass was utilizing for players, some statistics on positions bring a very clear vision of the fact that these kids in no way compare to college players or even high school players today. For his 1984 Newnan Cougars, here are some stats to look at.

1. Offensive line: The average height was six feet. The average weight was 205 pounds. They ranged from a 185-pound guard to a 264-pound tackle.
2. Running backs: The starting fullback weighed 169 pounds. The starting tailback was 154 pounds.
3. Defensive line: The average height was five feet eleven inches. The average weight was 190 pounds.

Not the size players we have grown accustomed to and not even that large for 1984.

In Newnan, Georgia, the paper of record was the *Newnan Times Herald*, and the main sportswriter was Johnny Brown. Johnny began writing for the *Newnan Times* in 1946 and was the mainstay of the sports section. During Max Bass's years, the two had a relationship that could be called a rough marriage. They both had respect for each other but at times, provided a few jabs to keep each other on point.

In mid-September of 1984, Johnny wrote an article that roughly said that Coach Bass needed to have a successful season in order to not get on the hot seat. Now, this was coming off two 7–4 seasons when they went to the playoffs and two years prior to the 1981 season when they went to the state championship. About a week later, Johnny placed in his column a letter that was written to him about his comments, and it truly gets right to the point.

Dear Mr. Brown,

Your article, dated September 20th, 1984, concerning Newnan High football was very interesting. This article echoed the comments I have heard in the past five years. I work in Newnan but live in Tallapoosa.

The comments concern Newnan not having a good year with a record of 7–3 or better. Criticism of not winning the big game in reference to the state title game with Warner Robins. Criticism of not scoring enough points, of scoring too many points, the color of the uniforms, etc.

These people are amazing! Or is the correct word JADED?

Success hasn't spoiled them yet, but it definitely has a foothold.

Tallapoosa's Haralson County High in comparison has recorded only one winning season in the past ten years. During this time, there have been two winless seasons of 0–10. The 10-year average is 2–8. There have also been four head coaches.

This is the other side of the coin I hope Newnan and my good friends never endure. Shudder to think what a losing season would do to the critics of 7–3. Newnan has it good. Enjoy it!

P.S. If the day arrives when the people of Newnan tire of Coach Bass and his winning ways, please call, we will dispatch a moving van to his door. Never again would Newnan TORTURE itself with his "bad teams" and "ugly uniforms!"

Now for all of you who don't agree, you can send $1.00 for purchase of a bus ticket to Tallapoosa. Send it to . . . just joshing, Hoss!"

But in 1984, the Johnny Brown Hoss Bass back and forth did not end there. In an article, Johnny decided to start off with the ever-changing uniforms of the Newnan Cougars to poke at Coach Bass.

Max Bass is in a profession that invites criticism, and the head football coach can only escape much of that by winning all of his games. Bass and his Cougars have already exceeded my expectations since they are undefeated and ranked fifth or sixth in the state, so I can hardly be critical of his coaching or the play of the players. Since he has not lost a game, now is the time to pick on him on an issue that has bothered me along with a few other fans. I'm talking about the school colors at Newnan High School. What are they? I know they used to be blue and gold and then were changed to white and gold or maybe white blue and gold. Then along came the harvest gold jersey joke, and from that we moved to burnt orange or Texas orange or auburn orange.

NEW COLORS ARE KHAKI AND RUST TRIMMED IN GRIFFIN GREEN

About an hour before Newnan took on Heritage at Conyers last Friday night, I was having my usual pregame argument with Bass, and the subject turned to school colors and how he has dictatorially changed those colors every time a good sale came along from a sporting goods salesman. I reminded him that in 1981, the Cougars were dressed in silver britches and silver helmets along with blues jerseys with white numbers or white jerseys with blue numbers. In 1982, the team trotted out in those awful-looking harvest gold uniforms, and this year, the team ran out on the field in khaki britches trimmed with a stripe of Texas orange and a stripe of riyal blue. I could tell he was not enjoying what I was saying, especially since he was worried about the upcoming kickoff with Heritage. He scowled, "Our colors are khaki and rust trimmed in Griffin Green."

The green trim is on the jersey, but Betty Rogers says, "But it's not supposed to be green; it's supposed to be a tan color."

Coach Betty tries to justify the actions of her boss, but she can't possibly be sure what the school colors are at this stage. If you will check the middle page or the roster page of your next Newnan High football program, you will see where it says the school colors are blue, gold, and white. Nowhere does it say anything about khaki, Griffin green, Texas orange, silver, harvest gold, or rust. Simply blue and gold and white!

I know this is a petty problem, and I shouldn't be picking on Bass about it. Usually, fans wait until Bass loses a game or two before they start picking on him, but he may not lose at this rate his Cougars are playing. Really, I agree with Bass when he says, "It ain't what color uniform you wear that counts. It's whether you win or lose." He will smile at you and say, "Why, I could dress 'em out in pastel, pink, and green as long as we win all our games!"

Bass is not humble when he is winning, and I hope he continues to be obnoxious, for that will mean the Cougars are rolling along in high cotton. I guess Bass has spoiled us over the years with his winning ways. He mentioned the other day that someone asked him if would we have another winning team. He reminded them that last year, the Cougars were 7–3, and he thought that constituted a winning season.

The fan responded, "No, I'm talking about playing for the state championship again!" Most schools would love to settle for a 7–3 record and somehow, we've accepted 7–3 as something just average. Sounds like I'm taking up for Bass, so I'd better stop this for now.

Before that season, Johnny Brown predicted that Newnan would be a 6–4 team. Then before the R. E. Lee game, Johnny predicted that Newnan would lose. The team ran on the field that night and broke through a sign showing Mr. Brown's prediction as, at that point, the Cougars were 5–0. Newnan upset R. E. Lee that night, and in the after-game jubilation, the players picked up Mr. Brown, carried him up the field, and made him ring the victory bell.

Smaller towns like Newnan have their own forms of entertainment, and the back and forth between Hoss Bass and Johnny Brown is still talked about to this day.

The 1984 season would not start slowly as Newnan would be taking on perennial power Warner Robbins. This was the team that Newnan lost to three years prior in the state championship. Warner Robbins was a highly rated team in 1984, and this game would be a State of Georgia highlight right up to kickoff. The game turned out to be a "kiss your sister finish." Both teams struggled on offense against each other's defense, and the game ended in a 14–14 tie. There was no such thing as overtime in high school football as well as college football in 1984.

Newnan would go on to win seven straight games and would bring a 7–0–1 record into the big showdown with Griffin, who was 8–0. The outcome of the Griffin game was a 35–20 victory for the Bears. Newnan would go on to win its last game, have an 8–1–1 record, and head to the playoffs. In the first round, Coach Bass's team defeated Morrow 14–0 and was ready to face the Griffin Bears in not only in the second round but also in the second game. This seemed to be a recurring pattern for Newnan, La Grange, and Griffin, as they were the top teams in 6AAAA. Coach Bass would say the first one doesn't count, only the second game, but unfortunately, the second matchup was eerily like the first and ended with a Newnan loss 35–21.

11 Newnan Cougars 1986–1990

Coach Bass was always one who said he and his coaches always need to be learning—going to clinics, talking to other coaches, anything that might give them a tidbit of information that could win a game. As such, Coach was invited to be a guest speaker at many clinics around the country. In late July 1986, he was invited to be a speaker at the Washington State Coaches Association. He spoke about defense, Wing-T offense, motivation, and summer workouts. While there, he got to visit with one of his players from his 1970s team, Drew Hill, as the Houston Oilers were playing the Seattle Seahawks. Drew was playing for the Oilers at the time. Coach yelled down to Drew, "See, I thought you were too small and too slow to play at this level." Drew did not get many offers to colleges, as many coaches thought this of him. Pepper Rodgers at Georgia Tech did give him that chance where Drew stood out as a wide receiver and kick returner. He had a very long and successful pro career as well.

Going into the 1986 season, Newnan again had to replace top players as well as coaches. It seemed that Coach Bass put together some great assistants who went on to coach at other places. Also, it was always hard at the high school level to repeat success every year, and 1986 would be no different.

The season opener would be against McIntosh, a good team, but not the challenge of regional 6AAAA play. Newnan won the game, 22–0, but to the coaches and the fans, it did not look like nor feel like a complete game. Coach Bass liked to make a point of getting younger players in the games to encourage them as well as get experience, and this should have been the type of opponent that would allow this. The fact is that by the end of September, the Cougars were 4–0 against lesser opponents, but he had been unable to put young players in the games because there just was not a separation of points in any of those games.

Newnan would win its next game and have a 5–0 record to start October, but the rest of the month would see a much different result in division play. The next game was North Clayton, and the Cougars lost, 22–7. When it was all over in the fall of 1986, Newnan would finish with a 6–4 record but, having lost four regional games, was out of the playoffs, ending a five-year streak.

The 1987 version of the Newnan Cougars looked a lot like the 1986 version, and the end result would look very similar. Again, Newnan started with a win over McIntosh, but by mid-October, Newnan would be 5–2 with a horrible loss to Griffin of 55–0. To have a team score fifty-five on a Max Bass defense was absolutely galling to him. Newnan would wind up 6–4, and even though they tied for a spot in the playoffs in the region, it was a four-way tie; Newnan was eliminated based on head-to-head wins. The one bright spot in the season was the final game where they upset La Grange, 27–18.

After two seasons of not getting to the playoffs, Coach Bass did what all good coaches do. "It's all my fault, and the buck stops with me. I've got to evaluate my coaching staff and see who is not doing the job and the same thing has to be done with the players. We can't make kids grow, but we can make them stronger with our weight program, and there are drills to help with quickness on both the offense and the defense."

After the 1986 and 1987 seasons, Coach Bass took some time to look back and rethink a lot of what he wanted to do. He wanted a program that not only won but had coaching that would help his players become better students, better young men, and better members of the community. To do this, he needed assistant coaches, and here is what he looked for:

1. He should be dedicated to working with young people.
2. He should be willing to work hard and make personal sacrifices.
3. He should be an honest person with integrity.
4. He should have a sound knowledge of all sports.
5. He should have a great deal of initiative and be ambitious.
6. He should be a sound thinker.
7. He should be tough mentally.
8. He should be organized.

"All coaches are hired as teachers first and coaches second. We must match up the teaching position that the school system has opened with coaches' qualifications and degrees," he said.

Coach Bass brought many principles of discipline and hard work to his program, and the improvement would be seen in his 1988 team. It also helped that his players were bigger, stronger, and quicker. In addition, he also had a star running back in the form of Eric Geter, who would go on to play with the Clemson Tigers and have a successful pro career.

Instead of opening the season with an easy game, the schedule had the opening game against one of their rivals, Griffin. One thing both Coach and his wife, Nancy, always remember about playing the Griffin Bears was the running onto the field by Griffin. They usually ran out of the mouth of a large bear statue to the sound of growling. Nancy said, "We always had to hear that bear when we played Griffin."

The opening game was a disappointing loss as Newnan fell 17–9 to Griffin. Starting 0–1 in the regional play is not good, but it does not mean that there weren't a lot more games to play. Newnan and Coach Bass relied on good defense and a strong running game and finished September with a 3–1 record. By the end of October, Newnan was 6–1 and looking at another run to the regional playoffs.

Everybody Needs A Mule

One of the hallmarks of a Max Bass offense was the occasional trick play. This could be a double reverse or something as simple as a fake punt. Usually, these would work, and the opposing coaches would be left just shaking their heads. Newnan had been working on a special trick play that would involve the quarterback throwing a pass that would bounce out to a waiting split end. The pass would be backward and behind the line of scrimmage, so it would remain a live ball. The receiver would then step back and throw the ball downfield to a running back out on a wheel route.

In Newnan's final game of the season, this play would be used. Prior to the game though, Coach Bass reviewed the play with the official so when they saw it, they would not blow the whistle. And just prior to running it, the officials were notified it was coming. Sure enough, the play unfolded, and while the other team thought the pass was incomplete, the receiver stepped back and threw the ball to a wide-open Eric Geter who scored a touchdown. Coach Max Bass struck again. No lights turned out or visitor locker room toilet paper missing, just a Max Bass original trick play.

For the 1988 season, the Newnan Cougars finished 9–1 and were headed again to the 6AAAA region playoffs. Things were back to normal after a few lesser seasons. The first regional game would be against Morrow, and as the game unfolded, the Newnan folks were feeling good. With just seven minutes, twenty-six seconds left to play in the game, Newnan and Coach Bass were up 17–6. But in all things football, the gods would frown on Newnan that night as Morrow inexplicably scored two touchdowns and a two-point conversion to win the game 20–17 and end Newnan's championship hopes. The team hung up their cleats but could still feel good about a final 9–2 record.

The Newnan football team of 1989 was looking to reload on the offense as Eric Geter had moved on as well as several offensive linemen. Coach Bass was not really sure how the season would go and would find out very quickly as they would again be starting with Griffin. Griffin was highly rated going into 1989, while Newnan was an unknown quantity. The start was a great one as the Cougars upset the Griffin Bears 19–14 in that early September game.

At the end of September, Newnan would be 3–1 and feeling pretty good about the rest of the season. October brought one more loss but three wins, including a victory over La Grange 27–14. Beating Griffin and La Grange set Coach Bass and his Cougars up with a chance to get into the regional playoffs. As it turned out, Newnan was in and, as such lost focus on their last two games and lost those. As is said before, with young men, it is hard to keep focus when you have achieved the goal that is first in line.

The playoff game was to be against Morrow, and even with a 6–4 record, Newnan knew they had a good chance to win. Unfortunately, Morrow proved the better team and won the game 21–0 and that would end the 1989 season.

The year 1990 was another season that brought disappointment. As stated, some teams would love to be able to say that they had a winning season, but for Max Bass, he didn't want to settle for that. The record would wind up 6–4, with no playoff, but it would be a season of what-ifs as two of the losses were in overtime games. The decade began like this, but his next few seasons would be seasons to remember.

12 Newnan Cougars 1991

Max Bass is a man of many talents and passions. Many who know him, including his wife and two children, say he is very tight with money and only spends on things that are needed. Another passion he has is like most folks in the South—he likes to fish. So, Max kept his eye out for the opportunity to find a piece of property in Newnan that he could get at a good price and that had a lake. The Basses lived in a very nice house that was close to Newnan High School, but Coach wanted something more. As fate and luck had always been kind to Coach Bass, he found his spot, which was twenty-two acres with fruit trees, a barn, a few cabins, and, of course, a very nice fishing lake. He got it at a great price and some years later would reconstruct the house that currently he and Nancy live in. Reconstruct because Max bought the house for four dollars and had it moved and rebuilt on the property. He calls his place Coach's Corner, and the long drive to the house is now an official county road called Coach's Drive.

The property and cabins did serve a purpose in the early days of his owning them. He would head out there with his assistant coaches for dinners on Wednesday evenings to go over any practice things and plans that they needed to close for the game coming on Friday. Food would usually be provided by the boosters, and the quiet setting would prove to be quite useful.

But Coach's Corner was not just for his own staff, as many times, the cabin was filled with college coaches on recruiting visits. One day at practice, Max looked over and saw two guys with green shirts on, watching his practice. After the practice, he walked over to them and asked who they were. They both said they were from Marshal University and had come to Georgia to scout for recruits. Coach Bass was going to have his coaches out for their usual Wednesday meeting and invited these two to come to the cabin. Fortuitous for all the boosters had provided huge steaks and the fixings, and the coaches ate and talked football. Coach Bass invited the Marshal scouts to stay at the cabin and offered the rooms anytime they needed them. As Coach would say, there were times he would come over, and a strange car would be parked at the cabin.

Some years later, Coach Bass was at a dinner where the new coach for the Georgia Bulldogs was introduced, Jim Donnan, who had been the Marshal head coach. Donnan stood up to start his speech and started with, "Where is Max Bass?" Coach Bass stood up, thinking he was about to be some kind of butt for a joke, but Donnan did not tell jokes.

"When I was coming to Georgia, I asked who would be the best contact for recruiting, and the answer I got was Max Bass. He not only knows his teams but can tell you about the best players on most every other team. But what I want to thank him for is when I was at Marshal, and my guys would come down here on a recruiting trip, Max was the only coach to set them up and take care of them."

Coming into the 1991 season, the Cougars would be relying on a lot of young players to step up and lead the team. During the spring practice, many players missed because they were playing other sports, such as baseball and track. Since Coach Bass was also the athletic director, he was good with this because it enabled his other sports to excel. The other benefit was he was able to really focus on many of the young players and work on their technique as well as knowledge of what he was trying to be accomplished.

Coach Bass had to replace linemen and a quarterback again, but for the 1991 season, the player they looked to take them to win was

Derrick Stegall. Stegall was an explosive runner and a very good passer who would help to offset some of the other losses. Fall camp was a trip to Timpouchee in Niceville, Florida, which meant contact, pads, and two days. It was the part of the season when all the cold ice tubbing took place. The season would start on August 30 with Morrow at Drake Stadium.

The schedule setup was good in that Newnan would play Morrow and Cedar Shoals, both non-regional games, before they got into regional play. When you are starting a lot of new players, having these types of games really helped to get them ready to compete for a region championship. In the opener, Newnan piled up the offense for a 35–26 win over Morrow. Next would be Cedar Shoals who was favored as they were ranked in the top five. The game looked like a Max Bass special as he told his players before the game that they would be "hooting and hollering after." And with a 17–7 defensive win, they got the opportunity to do so. Cedar Shoals was kind enough to fumble the ball five times, and they were all recovered by Newnan.

Game three was going to mean another opening with the opposing team running out of the bear to that growl as Newnan would be playing the Griffin Bears at Griffin. Griffin was 2–1 and, as usual, a tough out as Coach Bass had not beaten Griffin at Griffin in his twenty-five years at Newnan. While the Cougars were relying on younger players, Griffin was a much older team with twenty seniors and forty-three juniors on the team. Griffin was big and tough, but Newnan brought speed to the field. In the Newnan backfield was running back Corey Bridges who had been clocked in the forty-yard run at 4.2 seconds. Along with Steagall at 4.3 seconds, Newnan and Coach Bass had the quickest combination he had ever played with. The final result would be a Newnan victory 16–14 as Newnan utilized their two explosive weapons, and the defense did what it needed to get the win. The game was very important as with the win, Newnan was now 1–0 in the regional play.

The win over Griffin moved Newnan into a fifth place ranking in AAAA, but it was no time to rest as the next week, they would be on the road to face Troup County. Newnan, in its first three games, was utilizing its speed and quickness on offense as they were running the Wing-T. For those in 1991, not many teams were running this, but for Coach Bass, when something worked and was different, he was going to use it because it suited his personnel. The offense is a fairly simple offense that utilizes deception and option football to confuse the defense. Also, when you have fast-running backs and a powerful fullback, the offense can be very successful. For Coach Bass, though, like most things with him, he wanted to learn it better and, as usual, was at a coaching clinic at Villanova when that happened.

The coach was up trying to learn more about defense when he brought up the Wing-T offense and if those coaches knew much about it. They told Coach Bass that they were headed out to the University of Delaware where the offense was perfected and asked if Coach Bass wanted to go along. Of course, he did. Nancy was once asked if they had been to a town in Kentucky by some friends, and she replied, "Do they have a football team? If so, I am sure we have been there."

The next Friday night, Troup County saw the Wing-T in action and regretted it, falling 32–13 to Newnan. The Cougars ran the ball well, picking up 352 yards on the ground, and the defense, as always with a Max Bass team, held the opposition to thirteen points. The Cougars were now 4–0 and starting to look at a great season unfolding.

Newnan would go on to win its next four games over McIntosh, Henry County, Morrow, and Forest Park to post an 8–0 record. The offense was rolling up yards and points while the defense was being stingy as ever. Through those eight games, Newnan had scored 227 points while giving up only 82. But up next would be the also undefeated La Grange Grangers who were ranked number three on 4AAAA.

The La Grange game would mark a milestone for Coach Max Bass as it would be his three hundredth game as a head coach. In twenty-eight seasons, he amassed a record of 195–96–8 and was looking to make it 196. But Max Bass was not thinking about his record and instead was looking at facing possibly the best defense in the State of Georgia. He wanted this win because it would mean that Newnan would clinch first place in 4AAAA and secure a home game for the first round of the playoffs. What had the coach concerned was that through their first eight games, La Grange had not allowed any of their opposition to score more than seven points and had thrown three shutouts. His high-powered offense would have their work cut out for them that coming Friday night.

By halftime, La Grange was up 10–0, and the Granger fans were ready to pack it in and watch as they expected the fourth shutout of the season. But the second half belonged to Newnan as they scored fourteen points. But the game went to the Grangers as they scored ten more in the second half and ended up winning the game 20–14. Newnan and its coach were proud of the game they played, but for Max Bass, losing is losing,

Even with the loss, Newnan was headed for the playoffs, and they would host Mt. Zion at home in the first game. Behind a strong running game and a stout defense, Newnan won 24–13 and would move on to play their next opponent and, again, round two, Griffin. Newnan brought in a 9–1 record while Griffin was at 8–2, but like all rivalries, this one would be tough and even more so as the game would again be played at Griffin's home stadium.

The game was marked with big plays by both sides in the first half as Newnan took a 21–10 lead into the locker room. In their last meeting, Griffin had a strong second half, and Coach Bass remembered this and reminded his players. By the middle of the fourth quarter, the game looked out of reach for Griffin as Newnan was up 35–10. Coach Max Bass was not fond of what is called the prevent defense. The prevent defense is designed to keep all the passes thrown by the other team in front of you and thus prevent a long play, quick touchdown. He would much prefer attacking you on defense, but there is always the need to reason through your coaching decisions.

In the first game between the two teams, he went to the prevent defense, and Griffin scored twice to make the game closer. In this second game, Coach Bass put in the prevent defense as well, and Griffin scored twice to make the game closer. They still didn't win, but it was one of those items that Max Bass puts in his memory. But the story was that Newnan had gone to Griffin twice in a season and came away both times the victor. For Coach Bass, "When you beat Griffin twice in one season on their home field, you ought to win the State." Newnan would move on to another game with that goal in mind.

The next game would be against up-and-coming Bradwell down in Hinesville. Bradwell was 7–4 and looked to be a game that Newnan should win. But Coach had watched the films and saw not only an improving team but a team with big guys on both the offense and defensive line. The other factor was that the game would be played in Hinesville, which meant a pretty long road trip for Newnan. The game played out but with a different result than what the Cougars wanted. Bradwell took the win 21–16 and ended Newnan's run to the state championship. After the game, Coach Bass stated, "Getting up to play each week is not easy, but we had a chance to win and didn't get it done." Newnan would end the season at 10–2 but felt they left something out on the field that night.

13   Newnan CUGAS 1992

As coaches who played football grow older, the ailments and damage begin to show up, particularly for an active coach like Max Bass. He had begun to have knee problems that began to limit his ability to run around and to actually get off the field at halftime and at the end of the game. A knee operation was in his future, but in the meantime, it required some assistance.

The fieldhouse where the dressing room required a climb up a hill to get there from the field and, of course, a rush down to get onto the field. Starting in 1992, with his knee issue, Coach Bass decided he would draft his principal, Alan Wood, to have a golf cart available for halftime and at the end of the game. As in all things Max Bass, he had a decal put on the cart that read "CUGA," being a shortened southern version of the word Cougar. As this practice of riding the cart grew, the fans got involved and would cheer every time the cart made it up the hill. During a few games that involved rain-soaked fields, it was not always a guarantee that the cart would make it, so when it did, the roar from the crowd was louder. As always, the legend of Max Bass would endure.

After the 1991 season, it was clear to the coaching staff and the returning players that there was much to prove in the upcoming season. The Cougars would be returning an imposing backfield of Bridges, Steagall, and a very beefy offensive and defensive line that would include an offensive tackle at six feet eight inches and 320 pounds. The camp practice proved that the players were motivated and ready. An added twist was that on the way back to Newnan, the team practiced on the University of Auburn's AstroTurf practice field so that they could get accustomed to playing on that surface. This ability to use Auburn's facilities was due to Coach Bass's relationship with then Auburn head coach Pat Dye. Coach Dye and Coach Bass had spent several evenings over at Coach's Corner in one of the cabins talking football and fishing. Some of the teams they played now had turf fields, and their first game was going to be played on turf in the Georgia Dome.

The classic, as it is known, was going to premiere in 1992, with Newnan playing Southwest Dekalb in the first of a double header. The second game would feature Brookwood and McEachern. Coach Bass, in his style, decided to make this game a huge event for Newnan and, as such, dressed 156 players, which included all levels of high school, every cheerleader, and, of course, the band. The column of buses heading out of Newnan for Atlanta was at least a mile in length. But beyond the pageantry, Coach Bass knew he had to play the team that was second in the State Championship in AAAA the year before.

As the pundits looked at the upcoming season, Newnan was ranked number two in AAAA in the state, thanks in large part to the previous season and returning players. But like all coaches, Max Bass made sure that his players knew that they were nothing until they stepped on the field and won. "I saw them in practice Monday, and we stunk it up all over. I'm hoping they'll be down to earth and ready to play at the Dome, and I think they will," Coach Bass's commented to the press prior to the game.

The game, like many in 1992, was a Max Bass classic as Newnan defeated Southwest, 27–6. The Wing-T offense was running the ball, and the defense was shutting down the opposing team. Getting this first big win was important not only for the rest of the season but showed that Newnan was standing up to its lofty pre-season ranking.

Alexander would be the next game, and it would be the first home game. The Newnan faithful packed the Drake Stadium and saw their Cougars demolish the visitors 42–16. The sixteen points were late scores against the reserves as the first team defense held Alexander scoreless. What was an eye-opening stat in the game was that Newnan, running the ball, gained 463 yards, with Corey Bridges gaining 134 and Steagall with 144 yards. Steagall set a Newnan record with a rushing touchdown that covered ninety-nine yards on one play.

Coach Bass would be facing Morrow in the next game, but he was also looking at a milestone if they won. A victory would give him his two hundredth victory and place him as one of the winning coaches in the state. To win two hundred games is a number that not many coaches can claim. But as always, Coach shrugged that off and focused on the upcoming game. Newnan beat Morrow 29–9 and earned Coach that milestone.

Next was Douglas County, and again, the offense was explosive, and the defense crushing as the final was 34–6 Newnan. Coach Bass was never one to want to run up the score on another team out of respect and the fact that you may have to play them again the next year. So far, he had been able to pull many of his starters early in the third quarter in many games and play the younger players. In the Douglas County game, Newnan played one hundred players. "It's good to get them into the game and get them ready, so they know what to do. You never know when an injury will mean they are now the starter," said Coach Bass.

Carver of Columbus was next, and they suffered the same kind of resounding defeat, 42–7. Newnan, in fact, pulled its first string after the second quarter and played reserves the entire second half. The bad spot in the game was that Newnan had several personal foul penalties, primarily celebration penalties, and that did not sit well with Coach Bass. He had always taught his players to respect the other team, and he did not like to see any strutting or hotdogging after a good play or a touchdown. He said, "Youngsters see that stuff on the professional level, and they want to copy what they see. Pro football is a show, but we try to teach a team effort and develop character, and showing off after a big play is not what we like."

Troup County at home would be next, and again, Max Bass football, 28–0, would be the final. Corey Bridges took a handoff and went sixty-five yards on the game's first play, and that pretty much was it. Another game that saw the entire fourth quarter played by the reserves. McIntosh was next, and the result was a 46–0 victory. Newnan was now 7–0 and earning that number two ranking in AAAA. Through those seven games, the Newnan's first-team defense had only allowed seven points. All the other points were against the reserves.

Upson Lee and the victory, 48–25, brought Newnan to 8–0 and a big showdown game with La Grange. La Grange was in the middle of a twenty-three-game winning streak, as they were the AAAA champions from the year before. La Grange, like Griffin, was the rivalry game and, most years, decided the regional championship. This year, though, the game was a Newnan victory, 19–3. Coach Bass was not pleased with his offense but recognized that the La Grange defense was the best they had played all season and was just happy to come away with a huge victory.

East Coweta had never played Newnan as they had been in AA, and it just never worked out to schedule a game. It would seem to be a natural rivalry, playing the cross-town team, but for whatever reason, this would be the first year as East Coweta had to move up to AAAA and was in the region with Newnan. A win over the cross-town team would also make a new record for Newnan, as they had never been undefeated and untied in the regular season. The game was played at the Drake Stadium, and in the end, Newnan won and got that undefeated moniker with a 19–0 victory. Again, Coach Bass was proud of his team, but the lack of offense was disturbing him, considering the weapons he had.

Newnan was back in the state playoffs, and even Coach Bass felt that they had a good shot to go all the way and win it this time. The first game would be against Morrow at home, and Newnan won the game 33–7. It was a game again that saw numerous seconds and thirds playing. Next would be Colquitt County, and the 11–0 Cougars were looking forward to playing the surprising 7–4 team.

When you get to November in Georgia, you can run into all kinds of weather. As the leaves change and fall off the tree, you can have nice days with crisp cool nights, or it can turn quite cold with temperatures well below freezing at kickoff. Then there is a third option as those warm fronts come up from the south, and you get days of rain that soak the ground. It was the latter that proceeded the upcoming game, and since Newnan did not have a large indoor facility, much practice was limited to the gym. As fate would have it, the opposition got very little rain in their area and, as such, got in full preparation. To prepare for a game, you always have your staple of what you do, but if you are facing a team you have not played, you need to have your scout team run their offense and defense to get ready.

Newnan was fielding probably its best team ever under Max Bass, and the fans and players were looking forward to and expecting that twelfth win and the march to state to continue. But fate stepped in, and lack of preparation and Colquitt won the game 28–13 in a mammoth upset. As Coach said, when you lose, there are only excuses that don't matter. And, of course, you can only predict so far what a bunch of sixteen-, seventeen-, and eighteen-year-olds will do. But for 1992, the season was over, and with it would come the matriculation of much of its strength.

14   Newnan Cougars 1993

Newnan, Georgia, is a town that has approximately thirty-three thousand people in it and is the county seat for Coweta County. It is located about forty miles Southwest of Atlanta and about twenty miles Southwest of the Atlanta airport. It has a history of being a cotton mill town before and after the Civil War and was used primarily as a hospital for both Southern and Union soldiers. It has escaped any devastation from the war and boasts a collection of *ante bellum* homes, earning its sometimes name of the City of Homes. In the 1950s and 1960s, it grew in commerce and mill capability, attracting many doctors, lawyers, and other well-to-do folks, and at one point, in the 1970s, it was the richest per capita city in America.

When Coach Max Bass arrived in Newnan, the folks had not truly enjoyed a Friday night football game in years, and for most, the idea of beating La Grange and Griffin was not even relevant. During the 1966 season, Nancy traveled with Coach Bass to the away games, and while at one of these, she began to wonder why Newnan was always playing at someone else's homecoming game. She asked this of one of the other ladies she was with, and the reply was, "Because they think we can't beat them." Of course, during the 1966 season, this ended as Max Bass and Newnan won all six of the homecoming games, turning the tables on the other teams. It could be said that

Coach Bass was responsible for really messing up six homecoming dances as well.

It was not long before the Newnan football team brought excitement back to Newnan, and much of it was driven by the coach. His drive was not just winning, but he put a plan in action to get more community involvement in the program. He enlisted the First Baptist Church to provide buses to get folks to the game. The church also provided the pregame meal for the players. The booster club grew, and with it, other events such as the post-game meal that was provided by the parents and sometimes local restaurants, such as the famous Sprayberry's Barbecue.

Coach Max Bass put a lot into his team and a lot into his coaching and, at times, was so tired after the games that he didn't even want to drive. That was when, for some twenty years, he was driven to and from the games by Dr. Gene Tyre, the pastor at First Baptist. Dr. Tyre walked the sidelines with Coach and, at times, was even more worked up than Max. In fact, after one evening, Coach Bass and Dr. Tyre were on their way back to Newnan, and they both were so caught up in the football discussion that they missed the exit on I-85 and almost ended up in Atlanta before they turned around.

The 1993 season looked to be a rebuild for the Cougars as many of the players from the successful previous year had matriculated and gone on. Derick Steagall was now on the sidelines at Georgia Tech, and Corey Bridges was dressing out in black and garnet for the South Carolina Gamecocks. But there were still some very good players on the roster, and there was always the Max Bass aura and plan.

The year would again start out with the classic in the Georgia Dome. The opponent would be McEachern, and Newnan went into the game ranked fourth in AAAA. Coach Bass, as always, would bring his rock rib defense and rely on running the football out of his beloved Wing-T. For the Saturday game, the buses were packed, and the band made ready to pack the Georgia Dome and cheer on the Cougars. The game was tough, but the final score was Newnan, nineteen, and McEachern, seventeen. Coach Bass has won another season opener in the classic.

The 1993 season rolled out a lot like 1992 had with wins over Alexander, 28–7; Morrow, 28–6; Douglas County, 46–6; Carver of Columbus, 21–12; and Troup County, 13–8. Newnan, under Max Bass, was playing old-school football by shutting down the other teams and utilizing the running game to wear out the opposing defense. While not having the fast-skill players from the year before, the running game was powered by bruising fullback running mixed with some misdirection, the hallmark of the Wing-T offense. The opposing coaches knew Coach Bass would run the ball and were deploying eight and nine players in the box—close to the line of scrimmage—to try and stop Newnan. But once they did this enough, the plan would change, and Coach Bass would throw it over their heads just enough to get some big plays.

McIntosh was the next victim, falling 21–14 to Newnan, which had the Cougars, 7–0, and looking to get back into the playoffs. But all is not set in football nor right as rain, and on a very wet field, Newnan would lose to Upson Lee, 12–7, their first loss in the regional play. Meanwhile, on the other side of town, East Coweta was cruising along undefeated, and the game between the two, being in the same region in the AAAA, was looming larger.

But there was one more game to play before that final game and it was against rival La Grange. The La Grange game, like the Griffin game, was one that always brought out the fans and always featured a spirited contest. Again, the rains fell, and cold, rain-soaked stands and field saw the Newnan Cougars win, 17–3. The 8–1 Cougars now faced East Coweta at 9–0, and the loser would be eliminated from the regional playoffs.

East Coweta against Newnan was only happening for the second time, and this meeting held significant importance for both teams. East Coweta was extremely talented as recent redistricting of the school zones removed some areas from Newnan and put them into East Coweta's zone—kids that would have gone to Newnan now had to go to East Coweta. Also, the growth on the north side of the county was exploding as real estate development and housing attracted many new residents. Coach Bass said, "You can't recruit, so you have to play with what you got."

It was a very cool night when the two teams met at East Coweta's stadium, and the game would not go well for Newnan. A tough Indians defense held Newnan scoreless while they scored seventeen. The game ended with East Coweta winning 17–0, and for the first time in a while, the 8–2 Cougars were not heading for the playoffs, while East Coweta was. Many in the area now felt that the tide had changed and that the dominant Newnan team was in for a period of decline. Heading toward the 1994 season, it would be a challenge as the 1993 team was heavily senior-laden.

15 The Fellowship of Christian Athletes

Max Bass freely will tell you that much of his inspiration and development comes from his powerful belief in God and Jesus Christ. As a boy, he attended church with his family and, growing up on a farm, looked to God to direct him on his path in life. When he went off to college, one of his self-appointed tasks was to find a good church and attend every Sunday. Upon his arrival in Newnan, the Basses were blessed with help as Pastor Bob Baggott housed the family and, of course, inspired them to join the First Baptist Church there in Newnan.

Earlier in his time at Newnan, Coach had met Paul Anderson, the strongest man in the world at that time, at an event. Paul was a member of FCA and spoke highly of the organization and its merits and influence on young men. At the time, there was no FCA organization in the State of Georgia. After a few years, Coach Bass began to work with Pastor Bob Baggett and several other folks, including Coach Nick Hyder who was coaching in Rome at the time and would go on to be one of the winningest coaches at Valdosta. They were all interested in getting the FCA going in Georgia.

Black Mountain, North Carolina, is home to a lot of camps, and the Fellowship of Christian Athletes (FCA) is included in that list. In order to learn more about the group, Coach Bass worked with the Edwards Pie Company in Atlanta to fund a visit for himself and some other coaches. Once there, they were convinced of the value of the organization and returned to form the first chapter in the State of Georgia.

The FCA's mission is:

> *We pursue our vision and mission through the strategy of "to and through" the coach. We seek ministry first to coaches' hearts, marriages, and families. Then, when ready, we minister through coaches to their fellow coaches, teams, and athlete leaders.*

Billy Graham said, "A coach will impact more people in one year than the average person will in an entire lifetime." With the influence of a coach, FCA recognizes the most strategic way to reach more athletes is to reach first the coach.

The FCA is present in most of the schools in Georgia today and includes all denominations as well as boys and girls and women and men. Coach Bass said, "The FCA puts good kids all over the campus, and it just makes the school better."

FCA camps and meetings have proved a great place for Coach to meet with other great coaches, including Tom Landry, Grant Teaff, Mike Parker, Doug Barfield, and Bill Curry. FCA camp has also meant a lot to the kids who go, and as such to this day, Coach Bass still sponsors every athlete who wants to be a part of the organization that attends Newnan High School.

16 Newnan Cougars 1994

If you ask Coach who he admired the most and helped him grow personally and in his career, he would probably tell you, Jesus Christ. Then he would tell you Paul "Bear" Bryant. Coach Bass met the Bear at a clinic at the beginning of Max's coaching career. They were outside, and Max went up to him and introduced himself. Since that meeting, the two shared many breakfasts, lunches, and coaching sessions. When he and Nancy went to Tuscaloosa for a clinic or a visit, there was always someone there to meet them and a paid hotel room that always had cut fresh flowers for Nancy. What Coach Bass learned from the Bear was, in many ways, some of the most valuable lessons. On organization, the Bear said you need to have an organization in everything in your program. You need to have a plan for everything. Be ready for what could happen.

One day, Coach Bass visited Coach Bryant, and the Bear had, as most times, a yellow pad in front of him, and he was writing something. Coach Bass asked him, "What are you putting on that pad of paper?" The Bear said, "These are the players who will be starting for me in three years." Another time, the Bear had two pads in front of him, and Max asked him the same question. The answer: "Well, on this one, I am writing what I am going to say if we win, and on this one, I am writing what I'm going to say if we lose."

What the two coaches often spoke of, over a country breakfast, was their upbringing and where they were from. Opp, Alabama, and Morrow Bottom, Arkansas, are very similar as life there meant farming and being poor. Both coaches shared that beginning and that life is also what motivated them. The Bear is known for pushing himself, never wanting to fail, and having to return to life in the cotton fields. For Max Bass, it was the mule.

After announcing his retirement and coaching his final game in the Liberty Bowl, where Alabama beat Illinois, he walked away from football only to quickly succumb to heart failure and die less than five weeks later. For many, it was as if the Bear's purpose in life was done, and it was a sad day for Coach Bass as his mentor was now gone.

The 1994 version of the Newnan football team was going to look very different than the previous two years. Many of the stars were gone as well as experienced linemen. But high school football is just that way, and as Coach Bass said prior to the season, "We lost a lot of talent from last year, but you can't sit around and cry about it. The juniors and seniors will have to fill in and take up the slack." The slack was there as Newnan was returning with only one offensive lineman from the previous season; the rest had not started a game.

Like the last two years, Newnan was going to start the season in the classic and would be playing Brookwood High. The game was always big for Newnan and always packed buses heading north to Atlanta. It was also a moneymaker for all those involved, including Newnan High School. Much of the budget for a high school football team is acquired from ticket sales as well as concession sales.

The Cougars started the season ranked fifteenth in AAAA, but as with all preseason rankings, this was based on what the team had done the prior year. Coach Bass had never thought much of polls and rankings, saying, "Most of these polls are made by people who don't know any football at all, and they go on past experience and these kinds of things, and I imagine if you compared the first of this year like right now to what happens in the fall, it makes 'em all look like idiots." Coach Bass knew he would struggle in the first part of the season but felt after a few games, the team would get better. In the kickoff classic, Brookwood defeated Newnan 21–0. "We didn't play good offense, and we were not able to keep the football."

The following Friday, Newnan would play Lovejoy, and the game would be a loss for the Cougars, 14–13. It was an overtime loss where the winner was declared by penetration. For a while, overtime was decided by each team getting one possession, starting at the twenty-yard line, and whichever team sustained the longest drive would win. On this night, it was the visiting team Lovejoy. After the game, Coach Bass knew his squad was just not ready for regional play in the AAAA.

The next game would be the annual rival, Griffin. Griffin had a pretty good team going into 1994, and it would take the Newnan youngsters to really step up. The night was a miserable rainy night and worse still, the final score was a Griffin Bears victory, 20–0. The game just started bad for Newnan as Griffin ran a reverse play and scored on their first play from scrimmage.

Jonesboro was next, and fortunately for Newnan, they were not a very good team. But another night and the rain fell, slowing down both teams and causing many turnovers. The final did turn out to be a Cougar victory, 6–0. Next, it was cross-county rival East Coweta. East Coweta was fielding a very strong team and looked to be loaded with talent. As was pointed out, that side of the county was exploding with growth as well as benefiting from district lines being redrawn. After the contest, Newnan would drop to 1–4 as East Coweta prevailed, 21–3. After the game, Coach Bass commented, "We played as well as we can play. I think some of our kids are playing above their heads 'cause we don't have much talent."

Troup County was the next team up, and Coach Bass and Newnan had never lost to them. But there is always a first, and as such, Troup won the game 30–7. Upson Lee was the next loss, 23–7, and it looked like the season was coming apart. For Max Bass, this was a new experience, and while he and his coaches did their best, the team was just not as strong as those in the past. Youth and a lack of offense was killing them.

Carver of Columbus would be another loss, 27–3, and was worse than the final score. Fumbles and a total lack of being able to drive the ball on offense continued to put the defense in a situation where they just wore out. Coach Bass said after the game, "I've studied football, and when a team can make sustained drives, they can win football games. That is something we have not been able to do this year. We took the football and did it two or three times, and that the offense is getting better,"

The final home game was going to be La Grange, and the Grangers were looking forward to playing Newnan, which was now at 1–8. The youth and lack of offense showed again as La Grange downed Newnan, 17–7. A final road loss to Fayette County ended the 1994 season at 1–9 and was the worst record that Max Bass ever had in his coaching days.

17 1995: A New Chapter

Plowing behind a mule on the farm in Opp, Alabama, can put your life into a perspective that not many today can understand. While in ninth grade, Max's teacher gave the class the assignment to write a short essay on what they wanted to be when they grew up. By ninth grade, well, at least back in the 1950s and in Opp, you had faced a good bit of life and work, so you had a good idea of what you might become. Max Bass wrote in his essay that he wanted to be a football coach, and that day, the Lord must have read that essay because between Max's planning and the happenings in his life, he did just that—become a football coach.

Coach Bass looked at the 1994 season and, being a winning coach, did not like what he saw. He knew it would be a challenge as it was a team with much less talent and many younger players, but losing has no excuse. Coming into 1995, he was also facing a continual problem as he needed to replace several assistant coaches who had moved on. One of the tremendous measures of success for Coach Bass was that he had one hundred assistant coaches who moved on to be head coaches and top-level coordinators in college. The measure of any manager is getting their reports promoted. But Max needed these coaches before January, and the county was slow to allow him to get them hired. He was able to bring them on, but it was well into 1995, and spring practice was right around the corner.

Spring practice took place, and Coach Bass thought that his team looked pretty good but continued to be worried about the talent level and his coaches. He did not want a repeat of 1994, so he did some serious thinking about how to improve the team. But he was also thinking about other things as well.

Coach Bass would often quote his favorite coach, Bear Bryant, and one such quote that Max thought about was, "One thing Coach Bryant said is that if you can live without coaching, you probably don't need to be coaching anymore." After the spring practice, Max had a long conversation with his son, Vince, now a high school principal, and came to a conclusion that was shocking to Newnan, the school, and his staff. On May 30, 1995, Max Bass announced that he would be stepping down from being the coach, effective immediately.

As he was also the athletic director, he would stay on and complete his duties and his teaching duties until the end of the 1995 school year. He had also been selected to coach the Georgia All-stars in the Georgia-Florida All-star game, and he would do that as well. He said that the previous 1–9 season had nothing to do with his decision as he was just tired of all the duties that came with his job and just out of energy to rebuild a coaching staff. He was ready to spend more time with Nancy, do a lot more fishing, and just cut the grass on his twenty-two-acre homestead known as Coach's Corner.

A few months after he left, Coach the fighter did face a new opponent, one that did not have talent but had a mean streak. After putting off doctor's appointments to attend to coaching, Max went in for a colonoscopy, and the news was not good. He was diagnosed with colon cancer and faced some surgery and chemotherapy. The doctor told him that if he had not quit his job, Max probably would have never come in, and his cancer would be much worse. But as with all things in his life, the Lord was looking out for Coach, and Max had a full recovery. He even talked about being out on the riding lawn mower cutting the grass with the chemo pump attached, pumping in the juice.

Adversity was only another opponent, on and off the field, and being around good people, being positive, and trusting in the Lord was all Coach Max Bass. Whether it was knocking down running backs during his playing days at Jacksonville University or running up the hills at Drake field, Max Bass took on life with zeal, fortitude, and strength. He remained very active in the First Baptist Church in Newnan and the Fellowship of Christian Athletes. For the most part, he stayed away from Newnan football games because when he did attend, he threw a big shadow that he felt was not good for the current coaching staff.

He spent time with his kids, Vince and Beth, and his grandchildren. When you visit Coach Bass at home, you never know what ex-player, ex-coach, or state dignitary will either call or show up to talk to him. He was an avid reader as well as still a study of football. His den had three large TVs that he used to watch on Saturdays as well as on other days, replays of games from present and past years. His only real nemesis in his life was that in his fishing pond, there at Coach's Corner, a new resident had moved in—an alligator. Fairly rare to have an alligator in Newnan and he was not really sure how it got there, but for Coach Bass, it was his reminder to always be ready for what could happen to you. Always have a plan for everything.

Looking back on his coaching years, he did have one regret. "The one thing I regretted is that I have not been able to win a state championship." He was one game away from it in 1981 and got close in 1991 and 1992. But for that regret, the one thing that Coach Max Bass could say is, "But I feel like I have touched the lives of many of the young men who played for me down through the years." Coach Bass more than coached them, for many would tell you that he had changed their lives, and as many have gone on to great success in sports, business, and life, they attributed much of it to Coach Bass. In fact, Coach Bass did more than just for his football players as he was the athletic director and made sure that all the sports were taken care of. If the girls' track team needed new sweats, he made sure they got them, and if one of the girls wanted to keep those sweats at the end of the year, Coach Bass let them and replaced them with new ones for the following season. "I'm a hugger. I love the kids, all of them, not just the athletes. I'm going to miss every kid in school."

But in the end, Max Bass would always look back and remember that day on the farm when his uncle told him how good he looked behind that mule. And Max Bass never forgot and would tell you, "Everybody needs a mule."

Postscript

Before Coach Bass and I could finish this book, on January 22, 2022, he passed away in his sleep. He left behind a family of his two children and many grandchildren, along with Nancy, his wife. But what else would be left was thousands of adults who at one time were either coached by him or simply got a word of advice in the hall or the lunchroom, which would go on with them. So many of his ex-players and coaches attributed their success, not only in sports but in life, to Coach Max Bass.

I often said to people that if we could just get him in front of all the kids in America today, in ten years, we would no longer have any problems. The thing to remember about Coach Bass is not necessarily his football record and success; it is about how he had lived and tried to share that knowledge with anyone who would listen.

He was not just a Hall of Fame Coach; he was and remained a Hall of Fame Man.

Coach's Corner

Lessons on Life and Football
From Coach Max Bass

From 1974 to 1977, Coach Bass wrote a column in the *Newnan Times Herald* called Coach's Corner. The subject varied from football to life, but it truly was and is the insight of Coach Max Bass.

* * *

He Is Called a Coach

He is called "coach." It is a difficult job, and there is no clear way to succeed in it. One cannot copy another who is a winner, for there seems to be some subtle secret chemistry of personality that enables a person to lead successfully, and no one really knows what it is. Those who have succeeded and those who have failed represent all kinds, young and old, inexperienced and experienced, hard and soft, tough and gentle, good-natured and foul-tempered, proud and profane, articulate and inarticulate, even dedicated and casual. Most are dedicated, some more than others, but dedication alone is not enough. Some are smarter than others, but intelligence is not enough. All want to win, but some want to win more than others, and just wanting to win is not enough in any event. Even winning is often not enough. Losers almost always get fired, but winners get fired too.

He is out in the open, being judged publicly almost every day or night for six, seven, or eight months a year by those who may or may not be qualified to judge him. And every victory and every defeat is recorded constantly in print or on the air and periodically totaled up.

The coach has no place to hide. He cannot just let the job go for a while or do a bad job and assume no one will notice, as most of us can. He cannot satisfy everyone. Seldom can he even satisfy very many. Rarely can he even satisfy himself. If he wins once, he must win the next time too.

They plot victories and defeats, endure criticism from within and without. They neglect their families, travel endlessly, and live alone in a spotlight surrounded by others. Theirs may be the worst profession, unreasonably demanding and insecure, and full of unrelenting pressures. Why do they put up with it? Why do they do it? Having seen them hired and hailed as geniuses gaudy parties like press conferences and having seen them fired with pat phrases such as "fool" or "incompetent," I have wondered about them. Having seen them exultant in victory and depressed by defeat, I have sympathized with them. Having seen some broken by the job and others die from it, one is moved to admire them and to hope someday the world will learn to understand them.

Preface to Bill Libby's book, *The Coaches*

* * *

What a Person Believes

What a person believes has everything to do with what a person is and becomes. A simple statement of belief can describe so well a person and even a whole history of ideas. We hope that this creed may have special meaning to you.

> "I believe in the greatness of the individual and that I am in this world for a purpose, that purpose being to put back into life more than I have taken out.
>
> I believe in the integrity of other people, assured that they try as hard to follow the gleam, even as I.
>
> I believe in the gallantry of older people whose seasoned experience and steadfast devotion have preserved for me the precious heritage of the past.
>
> I believe in the magnificence of the past, knowing that without its storied wealth I would possess nothing.
>
> I believe in the challenge of the future, fully realizing there will be no future except it becomes alive through me.
>
> I believe in the contagion of health and that I can spread it through cheerfulness, wholesome habits, sensible expenditure of energies, and wise use of foods.
>
> I believe in the nobility of work as the creative expression of the best within me and as my share in easing the common load of all.

I believe in the enrichment of play and laughter as the means of cleansing my body of staleness and my soul of bitterness.

I believe in God. Who justifies all these beliefs? He is still the small voice within ever urging me towards the unattained. Since he cares for these things. I believe that even death cannot steal these precious possessions from me.

And whatever more I believe is entwined in those precious feelings that lie too deep for words."

—Anonymous

* * *

The Importance of Self-image

We are all thieves. I say this, men, because any person who does not believe in himself and use his God abilities is literally stealing from himself, from his loved ones, his team and the good people of our community who support our program. Since no one would knowingly steal from himself, it's obvious that those who steal from themselves do it unwittingly. Nevertheless, the crime is still serious because the loss is just as great as if it were deliberately done.

So the question is obvious: Are you ready to quit stealing from yourself? I believe most of you are. I believe if you have a good healthy self-image, you are ready to start. When your image improves, your performance improves. I read a story about a fellow named Victor Seribriahoff. At fifteen, his teachers told him he would never finish school and should drop out and try to find a trade. He took their advice, and for seventeen years, he followed their advice. At the age of thirty-two, he took a test, and it revealed he was a genius with an I.Q. of 161. Now then, he started acting like a genius. He wrote books, secured a number of patents for his inventions, and became a successful businessman.

Just how important is our self-image? Mildred Newman and Dr. Bernard Berkowitz, in their book, *How to be Your Own Best Friend*, ask a penetrating question, "If we cannot love ourselves, where will we draw our love from anyone else?" You can't give away something you don't have. The Bible says, "Love thy neighbor as thyself." The book *Born to Win* by Jongerwood and James points out that man was born to win, but we live in a negative world, and to join the successful parade, we must have a healthy self-image.

You will perform the way you see yourself. See yourself as a deserving person, a winner, and a great athlete, and you will perform this way. You have control of your image. Change it to the good side of everything. Picture yourself thinking and doing good.

Self-image

1. Look sharp. Have pride in yourself and what you do.
2. Hang around with people who are winners and good folks.
3. Know you can do anything anyone else can do. Jesus Christ said, "What I have done, you can also do an even greater work than these." He put not age, education, size, color, height or weight, or any other superficial qualifications as a requirement to attain this.
4. You are somebody because God doesn't take time to make a nobody. Don't care what others say as long as you are right and trying.
5. Carry yourself well. Smile, look successful.
6. Listen to successful people. Read about successful people.
7. Self-image is building self-confidence. One reason many people never attempt new things is their fear of failure. The person who has never made a mistake has never done anything.
8. Do things for somebody else. The greatest feeling in the world is when you help others.
9. Remember the victories, and don't dwell on your mistakes.
10. Turn off negative garbage. Be positive
11. Love people. Be too big to hate. I like what Booker T. Washington, the ex-slave who founded Tuskegee Institute, said, "I will permit no man to narrow and degrade my soul by making me hate him."

* * *

Letter from a Mother

Over the years, we have received many letters that we have cherished and been thankful for. A few years back, I received one from a player who wanted to quit on the field, and we pushed him on at the time and showed him he could go on. He wrote me from a foxhole in Vietnam, thanking us for showing him he could gather his guts together and keep going, and he felt this saved his life.

This is a letter received from a mother, which I want to publish because I feel that these are some of the things a player can receive from our program.

Dear Coach:

The football season is over, and our son has hung up his cleats and will report to another sport. Our school did not win the regional championship, but we win our share of the games played, and above all, our team won the respect of our opponents and our community by this fine sportsmanship and hard play. It was a very successful year for all and especially our son.

As a parent, Coach, I am eternally thankful that our son had the opportunity to play under your supervision and leadership. Each day during the football season, our son learned through example those fine moral and ethical character traits, which we all want our boys to know and follow. Thanks, Coach, for setting an example in proper conduct on and off the field. Our son tells us that you and your staff can be firm without being mean and boisterous, that you know when to sympathize, when to pat you on the shoulder, and how to correct you. These are leadership traits I want my son to acquire, and he can best learn these in the field of competition under the proper leadership.

For three months, Coach, our boy has really been under your complete control. He has adjusted his life to your suggested plan, meals, hours of sleep, social activities, etc., have all been adjusted to your schedule, and through these, he has learned voluntary obedience to rules in his scrimmage and games. He has further learned obedience to constituted authority. How much this obedience is needed in today's society.

Especially, Coach, I want to thank you for insisting that athletes study and keep up their grades. We appreciate you checking the report card and each grade period.

In conclusion, Coach, thanks again for all you have done for our son and the youth of this community. We appreciate you and want you to know that this is a better community because you chose the profession of coaching and the leadership of youth.

Your Friend,
A Mother

* * *

It's Worth It!

I believe appreciation is one of the single most important traits we can instill in our young people. Many players stand above the rest of the group. These players appreciate the opportunity to participate, and they appreciate their parents and their community.

I was told once, "Never to judge anyone, but you will be able to recognize the grabbers from the givers." A giver gives of himself, his time, service, talents, and possessions to God's plan. Our Booster Club people are givers.

This letter was written by an appreciative player.

> *Dear Booster Club Members:*
>
> *I was pleased to accept an award last Thursday night at the banquet. So the first thing I want to say is thanks to each of you. I'd like to take this opportunity to say something about the program you are supporting. In my opinion, athletics is the most rewarding activity our high school has to offer. The athletic program receives criticism from some athletes for its policies on such things as hair, training rule, and practices.*
>
> *Non-players ask, "Is it worth it?" I cannot express in words how much it is worth. It's the sacrifice that we make that makes it that way. These sacrifices set athletes apart from others and unite them. It gives them a feeling of brotherhood, which I guess only another team member can understand. It's a feeling that comes as the result of going through hard times together, and it can make any member of the team feel like crying without really knowing why. It's a feeling of love among the players. I wish I could explain this feeling better because, to me, it's the most important part of the program*

you're supporting. As it is, I guess I can only thank you for your support throughout the year and assure you that you're backing a worthwhile program.

Thanks,
An Athlete

* * *

Goals

At the beginning of this football season, I talked with our coaches about goals for their groups. We talked about goals we could set for ourselves. After this, we talked to our players and encouraged them to set goals in life, in football, and for the team.

As a boy, I lived near the Gulf of Mexico, and we fished and swam there often. I remember sitting and watching driftwood and trash in the Gulf, which were just sitting there and rocking with the tide but never going anywhere. I think this is what people without goals and direction do.

We ask our players these questions:

1. What do you want to become in life?
2. What are you going to do to get there?
3. When are you going to start?
4. In football, what do you want for the team?
5. What do you want for yourself?
6. How are you going to accomplish this goal?

When I was in high school, a civics teacher asked each member of the class to list three things we would like to become in life. I know one of those things I listed was "coach."

Most of our players had really not thought much about goals. If we help each of them find out what he wants to do and help him get there, we will make better young men of them.

* * *

The Inner Voice-Conscience

We in athletics have often wondered what makes one player have that burning desire to excel and others to be satisfied with mediocrity. I have found you can usually put players in three categories:

1. The ones who have the ability to succeed
2. The ones who have the ability and are satisfied just being on the team
3. The ones who don't have the ability but are going to work hard enough to excel in spite of their ability

It is my feeling that there is an inner conscience that moves all of us—the inner voice, the quiet spirit that abides within us.

Tom Seaver, the Mets' pitcher ace, phrased it well. When asked what his goals were for the coming season, he said, "I am not challenged by individuals, only myself. I don't aim to be another Bob Gibson or Sandy Koafax. I am a self-competitor. I set my own standards of excellence. Ten years from now, when I look back over my career, I won't measure myself by records or by other men. I only want to know that I was the best pitcher I could possibly have been."

Tom is saying that success is the ratio between what you do and what you are capable of doing, and that he seeks the approval of his own conscience.

King Soloman said it well, "Keep thy heart with all diligence for out of it are the issues of life" (Prov. 4:23).

George Washington advised, "Labor to keep alive in your breast that little spark of celestial fire called conscience."

We read in Galatians 6:4 (Living Bible), "Let everyone be sure that he is doing his best, for then he will have personal satisfaction of work well done and won't need to compare himself with someone else."

If we could open people up and look into them and see their inner conscience, we would know whom to play or whom to hire. These people who have this will be winners in all phases of life.

* * *

What Football Means to Me

There have been many variations of the meaning of football given by men who have studied and written about the game. These articles sometimes give a distant meaning to what a boy experiences when he actually plays the hard-hitting game. Football starts in the hottest part of the summer, and every boy suffers as much as he can be expected to at any time in his life. There is no doubt about it; football is the hardest work in the world. Each year, mothers and newspapermen moan and groan about boys getting hurt playing football, but they never seem to mention the thousands upon thousands of young people who are massacred on America's highways.

Football is a game of hard contact, and boys who usually have heat strokes and similar disturbances are boys who didn't consider doing any work in the preceding summer or either sat under an air conditioner.

Football needs men and not a mother's little baby. A boy isn't judged by how bad an injury he has but by how he performs with his injury. Scratches, cuts, and bruises appear each year, but the only one who usually moans about them are boys who want attention. Football becomes to a dedicated boy what a meal is to anyone else. Football has a moral and physical program for each boy, and the benefit is very, very great. To tackle, block and run hard is a form of food that thrills the player's soul to its greatest extent. There is no greater feeling in the world than to crack someone really hard and then get up.

Many boys don't put out their best at practice or games with a simple excuse. "Well, I'll be back next year, so I'll just wait until then to really hustle." Any of these boys might be in an accident and never play again. This is one reason every boy should give his best in every play of practice or game. Many boys can tell you that when you play your last football game, a certain joy will be taken from your life. Each boy who plays learns to love and respect his teammates because they have all been through the same things together. Even the boy on the bench hates to lose because he is a molded part of a group unity that works together with each practice and game.

We, the 1975 Newnan Cougars, have a chance to be better than any other Newnan High School AAA team in our town's history. Before us lie only a few days of practice and the game-deciding importance. When we look back on what we have already done, and even back to the hot August sun, don't you think that we can all, through a team effort, hustle a little harder for the next game?

If we do, we will be a group of boys who can look back years from now and remember that we were CHAMPS.

* * *

A Responsibility

Something that every athlete, at every level of competition, must realize is that although he may not ask for the burden of responsibility, he is an influence on those around him. That influence can be either displayed in a positive or negative direction. The self-discipline that athletics teaches us must constantly remind us of our leadership role.

To accept the advantage without the responsibility would be to disregard one of the vital lessons that athletic competition teaches.

Those of us who have enjoyed this role must never forget that in accepting the benefits, we also accept the responsibilities.

* * *

To Any Athlete

There are little eyes upon you.
And they're watching night and day.
There are little ears that quickly take in every word you say.
There are little hands all eager to do anything you do.
And a little boy who's dreaming of the day he'll be like you.
You're the little fellow's idol.
You're the wisest of the wise.
In his little mind about you, no suspicions ever rise.
He believes in you devoutly.
He will say and do, in your way.
When he's a grown-up like you.
There's a wide-eyed little fellow who believes you're always right.
And his ears are always open.
And he watches day and night.
You are setting an example every day in all you do.
For the little boy who's waiting to grow up to be like you.

* * *

The Fun of the Challenge

Challenging can be fun. Challenging may be exciting and even risky, but it can still be fun. More importantly, challenging is beneficial. It may result in losing as well as winning, but either way, it is the only route to progress, and progress provides personal growth and creates new opportunities for success and, of course, new challenges.

Often challenges come to us, and we have the choice of turning away or accepting the challenge and trying to overcome and succeed. We also have those opportunities that lie in the distance waiting for a challenger.

Surely, fear prevents many people from becoming challengers and, thus, cutting them off from success. Fear of losing, fear of criticism, fear of long hard work, fear of giving up personal comforts and routines, fear of losing some degree of basic security, and even fear of more aggressive people. All are possible obstacles.

Consider these counter-thoughts: losing won't make you a loser unless you quit trying. Criticism can't hurt you, and it's better to have tried and failed than to never have tried. Hard work that leads to a goal is never as attractive as the goal, but it's probably the only way to get there. Comfortable routines can lull us into non-activity when they should provide the time and atmosphere for planning the big move. There is no security on this earth, only in Christianity, and aggressive appearances by others are often just a show of force, and they still have to reprove themselves each time out. They can't beat you on their previous record.

To dodge challenges isolates us from opportunities to win but dodging also helps us fail. We miss personal growth, the confidence increase, the chance to fight alongside others, and the choice to make life better for many people as well as ourselves. Search out the resistance that will make you stronger. Locate the difficulties and obstacles that surround and hide good goals. Put aside the fears that are the real challenge—overcome your temptation to dodge the tough demands of progress. Don't feel secure and satisfied with less than your potential achievement.

Be a challenger. Have fun trying. Have fun going after success. Have fun growing. Have fun knowing that you went into the arena. You have to challenge to be in a position to keep on, and keeping on is winning.

* * *

Coaches' Wives

Last Thursday, as I drove to Atlanta at about 6:00 in the morning, I knew it was our twentieth wedding anniversary. I had made a deal with Nancy to take her out to eat Friday night, so I could spend the day helping with the All-Star game. I realized just how important an understanding woman is to any man's career. Coaching is hard enough with all the understanding in the world from a wife.

We spend our vacations visiting coaches or universities. This summer, we spent two days in Savannah looking up a rival team's coaches and films. Afterward, we went to Jacksonville where I coached football before coming to Newnan. After visiting St. Augustine, we wound up in Gainesville, Florida. Visiting Joe Kines, an ex-Newnan coach who is now the defensive coordinator at the University of Florida. While visiting the Okeefenokee Swamp, we saw another ex-Newnan coach, Fred Wilcocks, along with Waycross Coach Dale Williams and Ware County Coach Bruce Bennett. After four days on the road, we returned to Newnan and went back to work.

One week later, we attended the Fellowship of Christian Athletes Camp at Black Mountain. On the way, I stopped to talk to coaches at Western Carolina and interview a candidate for a teaching position at Newnan High School. Upon realizing we had to pass through Sylvia, North Carolina, we stopped to visit Babe Howel who I assisted in 1961 at Canton.

After leaving Sylvia, we went over to the Ridgecrest Camp for boys. The camp's director, Rich Johnson, was a basketball coach here in the late sixties, and his wife, Ellen, taught at Western.

We spent four days at the Black Mountain FCA Conference trying to find better ways to improve our youth.

The next week, I worked as a director to help put on the All-Star basketball and football games.

It takes a lot of patience to be a coach's wife. A friend once asked Nancy if we had ever been to the college where her husband taught. Nancy replied, "If there's a football team there, yes, we've probably been there." I've heard all my life that behind every successful man, there is a woman. I know I have been blessed. She cares for the kids, while I'm off working with others. She is the one who loves me enough to correct me when I need it and stand behind me—win or lose. She is the one who has to sit and listen to criticism at the football games.

For Nancy, and all of our coaches' wives, I know one day there will be a special place for you all for having to put up with this and us.

* * *

Top Three

When you evaluate the top three college teams in football in the national polls in 1975 (which are Oklahoma, Arizona State, and Alabama), what do you find as the ingredient that differs from the others?

1. Their coaches are all disciplinarians.
2. All run offenses that are disciplined offenses.
3. All players (backs) are required to block and carry their end of the load.
4. All are at the top in defense.
5. All are above average in the kicking game.
6. All can throw the football but are primarily teams oriented to running.
7. All have hard-working coaches who expect the same from their players.
8. All are perfectionists.

I believe the title of being a disciplinarian is the best compliment you can pay anyone. These coaches have done a great service for their schools and have instilled traits that will live with them forever. It is not easy in a permissive society to maintain these standards.

In our families, churches, teams, schools, businesses, or any other organization, if we take a look at the qualities that make these champions, we will see more success.

Young people respect and appreciate discipline. They may not tell you at the moment you administer it, but they will in time. One of the greatest moments for any coach is for his players to come back later and express how you helped them by disciplining them and showing them they could go that extra mile.

* * *

Tighten Up

Our football players this spring seem to have enjoyed almost every phase of spring training. We like this attitude and the atmosphere it creates during the spring. We know we have got to do certain things if we are going to have a good football team this fall. There are phases that I guess the players would say we have been loose on. When we come back this fall, these little disciplines must be tightened up and become automatic.

One phase of history that I can remember studying about, which most likely helped us all to be here today, was during the time of George Washington. In 1778, an unpaid volunteer Lieutenant General from the Prussian Army came to Valley Forge. What he found was a ragged group of farmers and storekeepers. This army was undisciplined and unorthodox, but General William Barron Von Steuben shaped this group. He was a perfectionist and demanded precision of movement. He also insisted on a neat and soldierly appearance for all ranks. In general, he disciplined. This caused many spectators to come and watch his drills.

It's believed that the troops could not have rallied time after time without this discipline.

I saw the same situation at the University of Alabama when Coach Bryant returned. This is one of the phases of the game that gives you a chance to win by not beating yourself.

* * *

Right Direction

The best teacher is an example. We usually reap what we sow.

* * *

Losers are Made, not Born

A father is many things to his son, but most of all teacher and idol.

A father—this teacher and idol—seeks ways to mold this smaller image of himself not into his own image but into someone his own man, unique, self-sufficient, and not a smudged carbon copy of someone else.

And one of the ways this teacher and idol knows and also explores to help his son reach manhood and maturity simultaneously is through sports.

For sports reveal to his son that life is a struggle, that skills to handle this struggle must be studied and learned and meshed with the skills of others so that what must be accomplished is accomplished.

Sports also shows his son that every struggle has an uncertain outcome, no matter what skills he commands. For in every contest, chance plays the starring role or calls, signals from the bench.

Sports show his son in telescoped time what his father most wants him to know.

The game is never over, no matter what the scoreboard reads, no matter what the clock says. The secret of the game is to do one's best, to persist and endure, and, as someone said, to strive to seek, to find, and not to yield.

* * *

Things are Looking Up

When many of us were in high school a few years ago, we were expected to choose sides with something that had a future. The person without a purpose or direction was looked upon as a bum and treated that way.

I believe we have run the course of hippies, dope, and "doing your own thing." None of these things have contributed to athletics or anything else. I believe the trend will return to where we expect more from all of our young people. I have always wanted to hang a sign in the lobby where each student could see it every day that reads, "Ask not what your school can do for you, but what you can do for your school." The students who participate in school receive much more from their education.

There is more to school than coming a few periods and getting a job to buy a car or just wasting a half day.

* * *

Hair

We have very few rules on our team. We can either treat them like eight-year-olds or young, maturing adults. It is their choice. Fortunately, our athletes have a great deal of pride, common sense, and self-discipline.

One rule we do have is hair should be well-groomed, off the collar, and no lower than the ear. Facial hair that is well-groomed and trimmed is acceptable. They have their God-given right to wear their hair as they desire, but team rights supersede individual rights. Their decision is not whether they want to wear their hair long or not; their decision is whether they want to join our team or not. If they decide to join it, then their decision on hair has already been made for them.

These are the reasons that have influenced our thinking on hair.

1. It is safe. He can get a better helmet fit when his hair is short; thereby, the game of football is safer.
2. We raise all of our money from this community through ticket sales and donations. This money comes from conservatives. The only people in this world who are conservatives are those who have something to conserve. Not one person has ever told me that long hair looks good. I want a distinct difference between athletes and potheads.
3. Short hair helps you win. Sometimes an athlete says that he should be allowed to wear long hair because short hair does not make him a better player. He may not miss practice and be a hard worker, but when he uses this excuse, hair is not the problem; hair is the issue. The problem is that he does not want to subjugate his welfare for the betterment of the team. He wants to be an individual, and you do not win championships with individuals.
4. I like short, clean, well-groomed hair. When they are head coaches, they can wear their hair long. When your hair is well-groomed, you look good, you feel good, and when you feel good, you perform well.
5. Over the years, we have found these people lack self-discipline. They are the ones who try drugs more often.

Our clubs, such as the Beta Club, Hi-Y Club, and other clubs, have high standards. All through history, the best of everything has had high standards. It is our feeling that a team without high standards will not win championships.

"Sloppy troops don't win wars," said George Patton.

* * *

Hanging Around with the Right Crowd.

It's been my feeling for years that if a youngster had the right influence, this would probably be the most important contribution to him being a sound citizen. We're kidding ourselves if we think we won't be influenced by our associating with the wrong crowd. Solomon, the wisest man who ever lived, married Philistine wives who worshipped idols. It wasn't long before his mind and judgment surrendered to them, and he started worshipping idols.

Last week, I was talking to a friend who has been very successful in raising three youngsters. He told me he had told one of his sons he could not bring a certain person home with him at an early age. This is the biggest problem we have in athletics: a youngster gets with negative thinking people and unambitious ones without direction. These people are insecure and want a group around them so they can talk others into going with them. We should be very concerned about whether they are surrounded by optimism, encouragement, and the right direction.

* * *

Thankful

When I think of the things I'm most thankful for, it has to be working with our youth.

I tell the players and students the most enjoyable thing I get out of life is helping people. I am very thankful that my job lets me be around and work with our youth. "He who gives a child a treat builds places on heaven's streets."

Jesus showed his feeling and saw the potential toward children in the way he spotted a child who was blind or lame in a busy crowd and the way he compared his own ministry to the job of children at play. The way he interrupted a serious session with his disciples, not only to take notice of the children who had come to him but to put one of them in the midst of the twelve and say, "Unless you become as a child, you cannot enter into the kingdom of Heaven."

Our hope is always that we may always recognize and help develop the potential in our great youth.

* * *

Use It or Lose It!

Every athlete should observe a daily program of resistive, stretching, and cardiovascular exercises all year round. The cliché, "Use it or lose it," applies to many of our possessions, our brains, cars, tools, and especially our bodies in athletics.

The body thrives on activity. Muscle strength can be maintained only through daily use. This also is true of our organs. When exercising, we pump blood to the stomach, pancreas, liver, kidneys, spleen, etc. This transmits oxygen and nutrients to every part of the body and carries off waste products.

The lack of exercise and blood circulation hampers the repair and maintenance of all body tissue.

The lack of regular exercise during the off-season causes a loss of strength and size in almost every muscle.

The lack of regular stretching exercises causes a loss of flexibility. For example, the hamstrings tighten up so that the athlete cannot place his palms flat on the floor while keeping his legs straight. The back also tightens up and makes it difficult to bend over, while the tightening of the heel causes a loss of spring and quick acceleration.

The athlete who doesn't do any running in the off-season will fail to maintain his cardiovascular conditioning and will substantially reduce his speed and endurance.

It's far better for the athlete to maintain his conditioning through the off-season than to rest and de-condition.

When I look back over my years of coaching, I cannot remember a player I've coached who went to college (and stayed and played) who was not really sold on some kind of weight program and workout the year round. A balanced workout program with weights, flexibility, and running is the most desired program. We like to include challenges and competition in ours.

Over the years, it has been my philosophy that we teach our players the program and encourage them to accept the responsibility to develop themselves. I'm convinced now that many athletes at this age do not accept this responsibility. We have decided we must do a better job of developing the athletes we have to the fullest extent. This, in turn, gives him a choice to get in our program and stay or get out.

In body development, there are no shortcuts or gimmicks. Many years ago, people worked physically each day and developed. There was no need for weight and workouts. Now people ride everywhere and do not do enough physical exercise to develop properly without some aids. I don't think it really makes a lot of difference where you work out or the equipment you use. The Russians have been winning weightlifting in the Olympics using stones to lift. Each year, someone comes out with what they call a better way of lifting, but again, all these are good only if the muscle is challenged through a full rating.

Back through the years, some coaches believed one would become muscle-bound. I've never in my sixteen years seen this problem. All the major groups of muscles should be worked. Our program works for certain groups one day and other groups another day. Flexibility exercise along with running is necessary.

Proper weightlifting and workouts will make the athletes bigger, stronger, and faster. There have been some sports in which lifting weights was slow to catch on because of some of these beliefs. All sports now lift weights to get bigger, faster, and stronger.

* * *

Live Right- Good Things Happen

Two weeks ago, I guess, was one of the lowest points in my life. We had planned to go camping at Rockridge Baptist Assembly and had just been informed that due to a mix-up on the schedule, the camp was not reserved for us. Because we were able to only go one week (August 17–22) during the year, the situation looked pretty bleak.

The thing that worried me most was that I had told fifty football players they were going to camp. Well, I had to find a camp, or it would look as though I lied to them. Several of the coaches had called earlier trying to find a place and were unable to find anything on such short notice. After about two hours of disappointment and trying to settle down from the time I knew for sure that we were not going back to Rockridge, I told the staff, "If you live right, good things will happen to you."

In a few days, we were accepted at Gordon Junior College in Barnesville. I've been associated with several camps in my fifteen years of coaching, but nothing like this place and the people there. What we wanted and the facilities were perfect. Gordon Military College had previously had football, the dressing room, training room, practice field, and weights, as well as the dorm rooms, which were more than we had hoped for. We were fed like kings. The classroom and lecture room for meetings and devotionals were excellent.

Time usually solves most problems. Overcoming disappointment is a problem for all. I tell our players there just comes a time in football and in life where you have just got to suck up your guts and go on. This was one of those times. Happily, I believe this may have been one of the best solutions that could have presented itself because everything worked out so well.

* * *

Trends in Offensive Football in the Last Three Years

Over the years, the team that has established a strong running game wins. This is true from the high school level all the way through pro football. To my knowledge, I've only seen one long-passing team win a championship. This was the Jets with Joe Namath who I think is the greatest passing quarterback to ever play the game. his year the Steelers won with a great running game and a short passing game.

The trend for the last few years in high school and college has been the triple option Wishbone and Veer with a running quarterback. The triple option football is changing the play with the quarterback while the play is in action. As the quarterback starts out on the play, he will have three options. The quarterback will read a defensive player, usually the tackle, to see what he is doing. If the tackle comes inside, the quarterback will pull the ball out of the fullback's arms and go on to his second read, which is the defensive end. If the defensive end comes after the quarterback, he will execute the second part of the option and pitch the ball. The third part of the option is if the quarterback is left free by the end, he will run the ball himself. If that tackle on the defensive side sits still or goes outside, the quarterback will give the ball to the fullback. Some of our passes are thrown off of a four-option action.

We are asked why we think this is an advantage offense. When you turn two football players loose and don't block them, this gives you an eleven-on-nine ratio. You have made the defense play your game in that to stop this offense, you have to assign people to stop certain people. You make them think, and if he fails to get the right person, the quarterback gets him the ball, and he runs free. Another thing, the defense can no longer back his ears and come after you. It's definitely a thinking man's offense. As coaches, when they stop one phase, we have got to know counter to move to it. This move is usually performed by taking one player from one area and giving up an area. Like the game of chess, we have got to take advantage of this weakness. The philosophy that I had when I first started coaching was that on Thursday, we, as coaches, had done all we could no longer applies. The coordination of the staff in the press box to the field is very vital to our plan. The coaches are assigned to look for and chart certain moves in one area and report this to the field.

Coaches, TV color men, and broadcasters are fond of telling us that football's triple-option offenses lose the ball more often on fumbles because of all that split-second ball handling by a quarterback on the move. This is not true. The fumble odds are virtually the same no matter what offense you use, based on a survey by the NCAA. The national three-year average was one lost fumble every 28.9 rushes. Triple option teams lost one fumble every 28.8 rushes, all others 29.0. The wishbone was the safest, losing only one fumble every 29.8 rushes. The Veer, 28.1.

A breakdown of points produced over a three-year period shows that the wishbone teams scored twenty-six points per game. Veer teams, 22.6, and others, 19.7

I don't think it takes a great coach to come up with what offense is the going thing.

One factor that we, as coaches, have to consider is, do we have the type of players to run a particular offense. If you are Notre Dame, Southern Cal, Ohio State, or Griffin, you could take those people and run junior high offense and win. I feel the triple-option offense gives the teams like Baylor, Clemson, and Newnan a chance to win.

* * *

Testaments of Coach Max Bass

Coach Max Bass was such an influence on me and hundreds of other people. He always talked about being a winner, a leader, and having pride and discipline in what we were doing. He preached about winners making commitments while losers make excuses. To me, he was larger than life. And I understand now that his greatness is attributed to how masterfully well he connected with people.

I recently looked at one of the Newnan High School-printed football programs from the 1987 season, complete with individual photos, position groups, coaches, team photos, and sponsor advertising. Down to every person shown in the program, one can see a sense of deep community pride in the team, in the school, and in the deep winning tradition that Coach Bass had led in creating. That was still before I got the opportunity to fulfill my childhood dream of playing for Coach and being a part of the Cougar family.

Growing up in Newnan and ever since I could remember, it seemed like every week, the local paper had an article covering the developments in the football team and included at least one photo of Coach Bass. His name and stories of his personality and sayings, and the hardworking winning culture he demanded at Newnan High were always a topic of discussion in the local barbershop and gyms that I visited. My ears were keenly attuned as I listened in awe and envisioned myself someday meeting and being coached by Coach Bass. He created a reputation of a winning culture, a football program, and a family that every little boy in the community hoped to someday be a part of. He used the game of football as a means to teach and preach character and discipline, and even hope, to young men. And by doing so, he positively impacted the lives of many, especially mine.

Unfortunately, my dreams of playing for Coach Bass were put on hold when I became seriously ill and was diagnosed with cancer in the spring of my eighth-grade year—at the time when many of my classmates were traveling to Newnan High School to start spring practice and then summer workouts with the football team. I continued to undergo treatments via chemotherapy over the course of my freshman year but signed up for weight training and went out for the ninth-grade team. It was in the weight training class that I finally got a chance to connect with Coach. He made me feel welcomed, in spite of my infirmities and the fact that I was so skinny and bald. More than that, he made me feel special because he let me know that he knew my great-uncle E. J. Jones, my paternal grandmother's brother. After making the connection, he affectionately gave me the nickname "E. J. Junior," which he would reference me by for the next two years. And at some point, he started calling me Vernon, which felt like a rite of passage to me.

Because of his influence, I loved the game of football, and I loved it so much that I walked on to play college football and toughed it out through three different head coaches at Georgia Tech. And after that, I kept pursuing the game that I loved, and it led me to play professionally in Germany, before ultimately landing opportunities in the National Football League with the San Francisco 49ers and the New York Football Giants. At every stop after my time at Newnan High School with Coach, the legend and name of Coach Max Bass followed me. From Atlanta, Georgia, to Germany to San Francisco, California, people knew the name and the legend of Coach Max Bass.

I am forever grateful for Coach Max Bass's influence on my life. And I have shared and hope to further share with others the gospel of a winning attitude, discipline, pride, commitment, work excellence, and others-centeredness, which he talked and walked.

Vernon Strickland
Newnan High School, 1987–1990

* * *

Max Bass Remembered

Max was a special person. He was very competitive. He would fish until dark so that he would catch more fish than you did. He loved people, life, and God. He could remember people's names. He loved walking around the court square in Newnan and talking to the people he met. On the week before a big game, he would tell everyone to come out and watch the Cougars play.

Max liked to eat, and he would eat lunch at 11:00 a.m. at Evans Middle School. Then he would head back to Newnan High School and eat lunch there. Then after lunch, he could be seen walking down the halls calling "sugar" to all the girls with a bread roll in each hand.

> Thank God for Max Bass.
> He was a great man.
> He was a great coach.
> He was a Christian.
> He was an American.
> Max was a great guy.
> Amen.

Hugh Maddux
Friend to Coach Bass

* * *

A Tribute to My High School Football Coach, Max Bass

The opportunity to play under high school football coach Max Bass and the Newnan High Tigers was without a doubt the turning point in my life. In those days, you either enrolled in college, worked at the local cotton mill, or joined the military. I absolutely could not afford college, and I had no interest in working in the mill. Therefore, my plan was to join the Marine Corps after high school, inspired by the Hollywood silver screen actors such as John Wayne, Lee Marvin, and Autie Murphy who starred in several military films. Due to some discipline problems at home, I was encouraged to live with my grandparents in rural Haralson, Georgia, and attend East Coweta High School. My grandparents lived on one hundred acres in an old farmhouse. It had well water, two potbelly stoves, no air conditioner, and a two-seater outhouse. Their home had no insulation and was dreadfully cold during the winter. I was up at 5:15 a.m. each school day and on the bus at 6:30 a.m. sharp as the first rider. This experience had a great impact on me in establishing a good, disciplined regiment and self-reliance. I chose to participate in both basketball and baseball, which, at that point in time, were the only sports available at East Coweta. During the off seasons, I worked with my grandfather on daily chores until dark and was in the bed by 8:00 p.m.

Now, getting to my football playing days. Following tenth grade, I had a chance encounter with Coach Max Bass and made a decision to move back to Newnan in order to play football for the Newnan High Tigers. My first experience playing football during my junior year was a learning process. I was classified as a migrant student, having moved back in with my mother in Newnan. Because of this rule, I could only play Junior Varsity. I was like a deer in the headlights that initial season.

Finally, my senior year began, and Coach Bass moved me to defensive end with Tim Williams opposite me. Paul Bass was my position coach and was the cousin of Head Coach Max Bass. Based on the obvious fact that I was a very inexperienced football player, the two coaches decided to employ an ingenious coaching decision. Instead of implementing the strategies that the colleges were doing that required cognitive thinking by experienced players, Coach Bass chose to simplify the instructions for Tim and me. Using his iconic Opp, Alabama lingo, he declared, "Beaucham and Williams, I want you to lay your ears back and tackle the man who has the football. Period! Nuff said! Is that clear?" This amazing stroke of genius turned us two boys loose to create much havoc and also made it a lot of fun! I would venture to say that the simplicity Coach Max Bass employed, along with the excellent defensive coaching of our position coach, Paul Bass, gave Tim Williams and me the freedom to attack the target, which was what ultimately earned me a football scholarship to Jacksonville State University in the great State of Alabama (not to the beaches of Florida where I originally thought Jacksonville State was located).

To understand the originality and practicality of the Max Bass discipline system, I'll describe one of his favorites. He called it "Gimme a Man!" When those three words pierced the air, we knew someone was missing blocks or giving less than 100 percent effort. A player (usually Tim Williams or me) would be summoned to tackle the transgressor from five to seven yards out as he stood on his toes with hands overhead on the whistle. Then there was the "Don't Miss Curfew Rule," which consisted of "the gauntlet" where the whole team lined up in pairs, and the curfew breaker had to run with a football through each pair of players until his exit at the end of the line. Needless to say, this consequence seldom had to be applied. I do remember a team member was caught breaking curfew when on a date with one of Newnan's beauty queens. Unfortunately, coach Bass just so happened to drive up behind this player on his way home from an event. Another mandate we all knew to follow was the "Do Not Miss Practice Rule." I don't remember this rule ever being broken; we did not have enough nerve to even think of committing that transgression!

I can speak of all this now as the Statute of Limitations has exceeded. Several team members have since become attorneys and have comically threatened to reciprocate! Coach always had an eye out for safety during every moment of practice, and we all knew he loved us. Most importantly, among the lessons we learned well from our beloved coach came from the "Don't Be a Quitter" sermon, which took place every day after practice. Quitting was the worst thing a player could do back in those days. I only remember one who "hung it up" during my tenure with Coach Bass. This valuable sermon paid off when I was a rookie at JSU during my freshman and sophomore years as it was very brutal in those days of "old school" college coaching. When practice got almost unbearable, I kept hearing a familiar voice in my mind. "Hoss, don't be a quitter! Suck your guts up and persevere!" Colleges then signed more than they really needed and weaned out the bunch to where only the strongest and most determined survived. I give thanks to the influence of Coach Bass as he instilled this philosophy into all of his players.

My high school senior season with coach Bass was quite a successful one for the team with a 9–1 record. The one mid-season loss was a heartbreaker to Lakeshore with the score being nine to seven. After that loss, the whole team thought we might not survive Monday's practice. We warmed up, and you could feel that we all had something to prove to our coach. We each were expecting the old "gut check practice" and, after some agility drills, engaged in a long, highly physical scrimmage. Our coach was so impressed with our effort that he called us up and bragged about us. That was smart coaching as we were killing each other, and we did have a game coming up Friday!

At the end of my senior year, Coach Bass informed me that I had a choice between Kansas State and Jacksonville State. At the recommendation of Coach Bass, I chose JSU as he thought I would get homesick and not like the Kansas weather. Of course, he was also an upstanding alumnus of JSU. Before the actual signing, I was telling everyone that I was headed to Jacksonville, Florida, where there were beaches and beautiful women everywhere. In reality at signing, I discovered that Jacksonville State University was located in Jacksonville, Alabama!

My two short of high school football under the leadership of Coach Max Bass and his staff was a blessing, and I thank God for having that opportunity. Coach Bass has helped hundreds of players to have the pleasure of playing college football and to get a college degree. Several of his players during his coaching career continued on to the NFL. Most important, though, he has helped thousands of young men to develop into good solid citizens. He taught us values and the goodness of self-discipline, hard work, and perseverance. He instilled in us the philosophy of never giving up and was a great role model through his passion for the sport of football and his service to high school athletics. If it had not been for Coach Max Bass, I would not have met my beautiful wife and had my two beautiful, amazing children. He made it possible for me to go on to make a living coaching a sport that I love so much. Hopefully, I have helped young people grow as he did. Coach Bass has been an influential role model, especially to young people for one-parent families, as was my case. I thank him for all the lessons of life he taught me and the great memories he made for me during those two short years of high school football. They have lasted a lifetime. Coach Máx Bass is a special man, and the Good Lord threw away the mole when He made him!

Thanks for everything, Coach!
Ronnie "Bad Cat" Beaucham

* * *

In Honor of Coach Max Bass

The local Baptist group has testimonials each week, testifying how Christ worked in their life. Here's my history and testimonial to a man who influenced me and others more than we ever realized: Baptist football coach, Max Bass. We might call him the Bear Bryant of Georgia High School football. Coach Bass inspired and motivated everyone he met.

My grandmother raised me until they sent me to boarding school. We used to play football in vacant lots with neighborhood kids. We would get into fights. Sometimes, I lost the fight. Other times, I would win. One kid got bruised more than me. His father was an attorney. They brought me before a juvenile judge. After that, they didn't let me play neighborhood football anymore.

I went out for the ninth-grade football team and tore a ligament in the last game of the season. I came back the next year for the varsity team with a new coach, Max Bass. Coach Bass didn't know I grew up without a father. He didn't know he was the nearest substitute, but he was.

I started on his varsity team, offensive, defensive, and kickoff teams, never getting a rest. Coach Bass took a team that hadn't won a game the previous season and turned it into a winning team in his first year. He was the game changer.

Coach Bass brought inspirational Christian speakers and athletes to school events and for his football team. He became the athletic director as well as head football coach. People were divided. Faculty and pompous academic types didn't like Coach Bass. Non-Christians especially didn't like him. They were legion. I was an atheist openly. I may not have realized it at the time, but Coach Bass treated me far better than anyone else, even though he knew I was very openly atheist.

Coach Bass was the rock-solid Christian. It took a decade later before I accepted Jesus as my Savior. In the meantime, Coach Bass saved me from things that I didn't even notice at the time. When they filmed the movie *Gridiron Gang*, they should have starred Max Bass, not Dwayne Johnson.

I used to instinctively say I played for Max Bass to people who had never heard of him or ever would know who he was. It just seemed natural to mention it. It was like General Patton's soldiers saying they served under Patton.

Coach Bass was a major highlight in my life. Now he's about twenty minutes from Atlanta.

I played three seasons, starting defensive end in high school. I went on and played varsity starting middle linebacker in college during my freshman year. Then I went into the military, Army infantry, and a war zone. Looking back, I'd have to credit Coach Bass for my college football and military success. But more importantly, I would credit Coach Bass for my finally becoming a Christian. It did take ten years, but it happened. He made the difference. Many "Christians" turned me off to Christianity, but Coach Max Bass was very different.

Coach Bass has been sighted at the First Baptist Church of Newnan, Georgia. He's retired now, honored by the Georgia Senate, and inducted into the Hall of Fame. Coach Bass inspired thousands. Anyone who played for him will always remember him. God worked through him, more than we realized, more than Coach Bass realizes.

Coach Bass was the first president of the Georgia Fellowship of Christian Athletes, with one of the largest chapters in the state.

Written by one of Coach Bass's former football players

Photo Gallery

Photogallery

Max Bass with his father Luther, his momma
Callie, his brothers Loyal and Bobby.

Football playing days at Jacksonville State University

Nancy and Max at the dance Jacksonville State 1958

Max Bass and Nancy at their wedding August 2nd, 1959

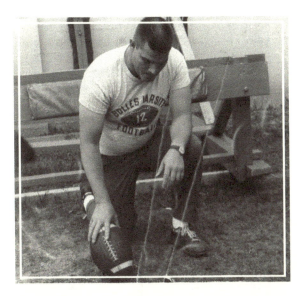

Head Coach Bass at the Bolles School Jacksonville, Florida

Newnan High school, Coach Bass getting ready to send in the play

Another victory for the Newnan Cougars and Coach Bass

Friday night football with his son Vince

One hundred wins in the books celebrated with Nancy, Vince and daughter Beth.

Coach Bass on the sidelines thinking up defensive strategy

Head coach Bass watching his offense in action

Another tough practice

The infamous golf cart to take coach up the hill at the half

After retirement Coach doing what he loved, working his land

Coach Bass off for a drive around Coach's Corner

Coach Bass with grandchildren Jessica, Callie, Tripp, and Wallace

Coach and Nancy in Alaska

Coach and Nancy with old friends from Jacksonville State.

Coach Bass with former players and coaches.

Hall of Fame induction

The Bass family at the hall of fame induction

Coach Basses daughter Beth with children Lauren, Jessica, Courtney, Eric, Tripp, and John

Vince Bass with Callie, Laura, and Wallace

Coach Max Bass at his home, Coaches Corner.